THE
REINCARNATION
LIBRARY

Written words can do no more than recall the things of which they treat to the mind of one who knows them already.

PLATO. *Phaedrus*

Wisdom is One

BEING A COLLECTION OF QUOTATIONS FROM
THE SAYINGS AND WRITINGS OF SOME OF
THE MASTERS AND THEIR FOLLOWERS,
COLLATED TO SHOW THE FUNDAMENTAL
IDENTITY OF ALL VERITABLE TEACHINGS

COMPILED BY

B. W. Huntsman

AEON PUBLISHING COMPANY

MAMARONECK

NEW YORK

Contents

Ignorance and Error

The Choice of Ways

Awakening and Revaluation

Self-Control

Action

True Teachers

Evolution and Attainment

Foreword

THROUGH all the ages and in many lands have been those who spoke with the authority of their own experience on the fundamental questions of life. They gave their teaching, to those who listened, by word of mouth; and it was very seldom that any great teacher himself set down his teaching in writing. The records of their sayings, therefore, are usually to be found only in the writings of their followers, or in the scriptures of religious systems which came after them. The exact meaning of the Master's original words is thus liable to be obscured; and it has often been further clouded by the difficulties of translation. In spite of this, a very valuable heritage has come down to us in writing from the past.

Although we find that the phraseology of their sayings varied of course with the period and the country, and that emphasis was often laid on different facets—Jesus, for example, stressed the need for humility, whilst Zoroaster insisted upon purity—in their essentials all these veritable teachings were identical, for that which is true must have been always and will be for all time; and the foundations of all true religions must be the same.

The following quotations have been collated in an attempt to show the similarity of the sayings, and to illustrate, as far as necessarily brief quotations will allow, the fundamentals of all true teachings: —that law does govern all, and that nothing can happen to us but what we ourselves have made possible and necessary; that there is a definite and well-ordered plan for the evolution of spirit; that the individual spirit, using soul, the vehicle of thought and feeling, and body, the vehicle of action, comes to Earth each time as to a day in school; that each individual must work out his own perfection; and that, by the right use of one's own free-will and by one's own experience, perfection can and will be attained—the attainment ensuring freedom from the wheel of birth and death on Earth.

The Law of Karma

1

Karma: Reaping as One Sows

1. With the same measure that ye mete withal it shall be measured to you again.

JESUS.   Luke vi, 38.

2. Be not deceived; God is not mocked: for whatsoever a man soweth, that shall he also reap.

PAUL.   Galatians vi, 7.

3. Light is sown for the righteous.

Psalm xcvii, 11.

4. Say ye of the righteous, that it shall be well with him: for they shall eat the fruit of their doings.

Isaiah iii, 10 (R.V.).

5. Glorious is the fruit of good labours.

Wisdom of Solomon iii, 15.

6. It lies within ourselves and in our own actions to possess either happiness or holiness; or by sloth and negligence to fall from happiness into wickedness and ruin.

ORIGEN.   De Principiis, i, v, 5.

7. For all the unjust deeds that each man has ever done, and for all the men to whom he has done injustice, he pays the penalty in due course.

PLATO.   The Republic, x, 13.

8. The natural properties and privileges of a reasonable soul are: . . . that she reaps her own fruits whatsoever.

MARCUS AURELIUS. *Meditations*, xi, 1.

9. He bestoweth wickedness on him that worketh wickedness, and right and truth upon him that worketh right and truth.

The Egyptian Book of the Dead, xvii, 29.

10. Heaven is sure to give happiness to those who love and benefit other men, and is sure to bring calamities on those who hate and maltreat other men.

Mo Tse, iv.

11. Happiness and misfortune are indeed always of man's own seeking.

Mencius, iii, 4.

12. The good and bad fortune of man are not predestined; man brings them on himself by his conduct. The consequences of good and evil follow as the shadow follows the body.

Kan Ying Phien, i.

13. Act maketh joy and woe. What hath been bringeth what shall be.

THE BUDDHA. *The Light of Asia*, viii.

14. One's deeds are not lost, they will surely come back to you.

Sutta-Nipata, iii, 10, 10.

15. Actions receive their rewards; and our deeds have their results.

Vinaya, Mahavagga, i, 38, 11.

16. Happiness and misery will depend upon Karma.

The Tibetan Book of the Dead, ii, 1.

17. Every good deed will bear its fruit to men; there is no escape from the effect of one's actions.

Uttaradhyayana-Sutra, xiii, 10 (*Jainism*).

18. Who hath not reaped what he hath sown? Wheat springeth from wheat and barley from barley.

Banda, v, 254 (*Sikhism*).

19. Honey the winds pour forth for the righteous.

Rig Veda, i, 90, 6.

20. Whoever has qualities is the doer of deeds that bring recompense; and of such action surely he experiences the consequence.

Svetasvatara Upanishad, v, 7.

21. Thou canst not gather what thou didst not sow; as thou dost plant the tree so will it grow.

Laws of Manu, ix, 40.

22. The fruit of Soothfastness is true and sweet; the fruit of lusts is pain and toil; the fruit of Ignorance is deeper darkness.

KRISHNA. *Bhagavad-Gita*, xiv, 16.

2

Misfortune is the Result of One's Own Actions

1. Woe unto the world because of offences, for it must needs be that offences come; but woe to that man by whom the offence cometh.

JESUS. Matthew xviii, 7.

2. If any man shall kill with the sword, with the sword must he be killed.

Revelation xiii, 10 (R.V.).

3. They that plow iniquity and sow trouble, reap the same.

Job iv, 8 (R.V.).

4. Everyone shall die for his own iniquity: every man that eateth the sour grape, his teeth shall be set on edge.

Jeremiah xxxi, 30.

5. They have sown the wind, and they shall reap the whirlwind.

Hosea viii, 7.

6. So Christiana's boys, as boys are apt to do, being pleased with the trees, and with the fruit that did hang thereon, did plash them, and began to eat. . . . Now Matthew, the eldest son of Christiana, fell sick.

JOHN BUNYAN. Pilgrim's Progress, Part 2.

7. With you the occasion, as with you the fault.

DANTE. *Purgatorio*, xvi, 19.

8. Man being sick in body and soul, this mortal sickness must have a cause, and this cause is to be found in the very matter out of which he is made . . . the ferment of sin is in us; in this ferment human corruption originates.

ECKARTSHAUSEN. *The Cloud upon the Sanctuary*, v.

9. Men possess self-chosen woes.

Golden Verses of the Pythagoreans, 54.

10. All things which come from the hands of the gods are as good as they can be, except perhaps for some evil which has been necessitated by sin in a previous existence.

PLATO. *The Republic*, x, 12.

11. The unjust conduct of one man towards another is indeed unjust to the doer, and the agent is not without blame, yet being co-ordinated in the universe, it is not unjust with reference to it, nor to him who suffers the injury, but it is thus fit that it should take place. . . . For this co-ordination of things is accurate in the retribution of that which is appropriate.

PLOTINUS. *Ennead*, iv, 3, 16.

12. Of evil we ourselves are the authors, since it is we who made choice of it.

It is not the anger of the gods that injures us, but our own ignorance of their nature.

PORPHYRY. *Letter to Marcella*, viii and xvi.

13. He who wandereth from the straightest path, in his inmost heart hath sorrow.

ZARATHUSHTRA.   *The Avesta, Yasht,* x, 105.

14. The man who transgresses the behests of Maät is sorely punished.

The Teaching of Ptah-hotep, v.

15. He who is headstrong and violent, shall meet a violent death.

LAO TSE.   *Tao Teh King,* xlii.

16. Beware, beware! your actions will recoil on your own head.

TSENG-TZE.   *Mencius,* ii, 12.

17. If a man speaks or acts with an evil thought, pain follows him, as the wheel follows the foot of the ox that draws the carriage.

Dhammapada, i.

18. Whatever pain arises is all in consequence of craving, but from the complete destruction of craving, through absence of passion, there is no origin of pain.

THE BUDDHA.   *Sutta-Nipata,* iii, 12, 16.

19. That thou art suffering so cometh from thine own karma; it is not due to anyone else's: it is thine own karma.

The Tibetan Book of the Dead, ii, 1.

20. In this world living beings suffer individually for their deeds; for the deed they themselves have done they obtain punishment, and will not get over it before they have felt it.

Sutra-Kritanga, i, 2, 14 (*Jainism*).

21. Thy woe and weal are according to thine acts.

Trilochan, vi, 80 (*Sikhism*).

3

The Law will see to Justice

1. Vengeance is mine; I will repay, saith the Lord.

PAUL.   *Romans* xii, 19.

2. God is faithful, who will not suffer you to be tempted above that ye are able.

PAUL.   1 *Corinthians* x, 13.

3. To me belongeth vengeance and recompense.

Deuteronomy xxxii, 35.

4. I will render to the man according to his work.

Proverbs xxiv, 29.

5. If thou seest the oppression of the poor, and violent perverting of judgment and justice in a province, marvel not at the matter: for he that is higher than the highest regardeth; and there be higher than they.

Ecclesiastes v, 8.

6. Three things it is impossible God should not perform: what is most beneficial, what is most needful, and what is most beautiful.

Welsh Triad.

7. The Essenes affirm that Fate governs all things, and that nothing befalls men but what is according to its determination.

JOSEPHUS.   *Antiquities of the Jews*, xiii, 5, 9.

8. And this is the cause of the diversity among rational creatures, deriving its origin not from the will or judgment of the Creator, but from the freedom of the individual will. . . . On which account the Creator will neither appear to be unjust in distributing to everyone according to his merits; nor will the happiness or unhappiness of each one's birth, or whatever be the condition that falls to his lot, be deemed accidental.

ORIGEN. *De Principiis*, 2, ix, 6.

9. O Zeus . . . along the noiseless path Thou treadest all mortal things are guided in the way of Justice.

EURIPIDES.

10. To suffer for one's faults is a deliverance from injustice and wrong-doing.

PLATO. *Gorgias* (479).

11. Whatsoever doth happen in the world, doth happen justly, and so if thou doest well take heed, thou shalt find it. I say not only in right order by a series of inevitable consequences, but according to justice and as it were by way of equal distribution, according to the true worth of everything.

MARCUS AURELIUS. *Meditations*, iv, 8.

12. No one can ever fly from the punishment which it becomes him to suffer for unjust deeds. For the divine law is inevitable. . . . In the law it is promulgated how much and how long it is necessary to suffer.

PLOTINUS. *Ennead*, iv, 3, 24.

13. Thou [Mazda] hast rewards for deeds and words, and hast given evil to the bad and good to the good.

ZARATHUSHTRA. *The Avesta, Yasna*, xliii, 5.

14. It is the Almighty who advances the seat of him that is advanced. It is not effected by the force of man.

The Teaching of Ptah-hotep, xiii.

15. Heaven and earth are impartial, they regard all creatures as sacred.

LAO TSE. *Tao Teh King*, v.

16. What heaven appoints is without error.

Shu King, iv, 3.

17. Heaven, as it gives life to all creatures, can surely be trusted to give to each what is due to its basic capacity. And thus it is that the well-planted is nourished and the ill-planted falls prostrate.

TZU SSU. *The Doctrine of the Mean*, 17.

18. I am alike for all. I know not hate, I know not favour.

KRISHNA. *Bhagavad-Gita*, ix, 29.

4

Not Interfering with Others

1. Judge not, and ye shall not be judged; condemn not, and ye shall not be condemned.

JESUS.   *Luke* vi, 37.

2. There is one lawgiver, who is able to save and to destroy: who art thou that judgest another?

James iv, 12.

3. If thou meddle much, thou shalt not be innocent.

Ecclesiasticus xi, 10.

4. They neither reprove other men's lives, nor glory in their own.

SIR THOMAS MORE.   *Utopia*, Book II.

5. To mind one's own business and not to be meddlesome is justice.

PLATO.   *The Republic*, iv, 11.

6. The divine law: To hold fast that which is his own, and to claim nothing that is another's.

EPICTETUS.   *Dissertations*, ii, 16.

7. Meddle not with many things, if thou wilt live cheerfully. Certainly there is nothing better than for a man to confine himself to necessary actions.

Another man's sin. Why should it trouble thee? Let him look to it, whose sin it is.

MARCUS AURELIUS. *Meditations,* iv, 20; ix, 18.

8. Thou shouldst not be too much arranging the world; for the world-arranging man becomes spirit-destroying.

Menog-i Khrad, ii, 100 (*Zoroastrianism*).

9. The noisy, hot-headed man in his hour ... leave the matter of him to the God who knows how to requite him.

The Teaching of Amen-em-apt, 90–92.

10. The more restrictive the laws, the poorer the people. The more the laws are in evidence, the more do thieves and robbers abound.

LAO TSE. *Tao Teh King,* lvii.

11. The disease of men is this: that they neglect their own fields and go to weed the fields of others.

Mencius, vii, 2, 32.

12. The perfect man of old was first concerned about himself before he started being concerned about others.

Kwang Tse, iv, 1.

13. Do not call attention to the faults of others.

Kan Ying Phien, 3.

14. The man of principle ... whilst he loves men to be good, does not push them to it; whilst he hates men being bad, he does not get wrought up about it.

TSENG SHEN. *Ta Tai Li*, xlix.

15. The fault of others is easily perceived, but that of oneself is difficult to perceive; a man winnows his neighbour's faults like chaff, but his own fault he hides.

Dhammapada, 252.

16. He is not a friend who always eagerly suspects a breach and looks out for faults.

Sutta-Nipata, ii, 3, 3.

17. It is better to do one's own task, though imperfectly, than to do another's, even though well-performed.

KRISHNA. *Bhagavad-Gita*, iii, 35.

5

Treating Others as Oneself

1. All things whatsoever ye would that men should do to you, do ye even so to them: for this is the law and the prophets.

JESUS.   *Matthew* vii, 12.

2. For the whole law is fulfilled in one word, even in this: Thou shalt love thy neighbour as thyself.

PAUL.   *Galatians* v, 14 (R.*V*.).

3. Thou shalt not hate thy brother in thine heart . . . but thou shalt love thy neighbour as thyself.

Leviticus xix, 17–18.

4. Consider thy neighbour's liking by thine own.

Ecclesiasticus xxxi, 15 (R.*V*.).

5. Now the Way of Life is this: first, thou shalt love God who made thee; secondly, thy neighbour as thyself; and all things whatsoever thou wouldst not have done to thee, neither do thou to another.

The Didache, i, 2.

6. Three laws of man's actions: what he forbids in another, what he requires from another, what he cares not how it is done by another.

Welsh Triad.

7. The spiritual life consists in loving God above everything, and your neighbour as yourself. In this twofold love consists the principle of the new life.

ECKARTSHAUSEN.   *The Cloud upon the Sanctuary*, vi.

8. That which thou wouldst not suffer thyself, seek not to lay upon others. Thou wouldst not be a slave—look to it, that others be not slaves to thee.

EPICTETUS.   *Fragments*, xliii.

9. Do not unto others all that which is not well for oneself.

Shayast-na-shayast, xiii, 29 (*Zoroastrianism*).

10. The treatment which you do not like for yourself you must not hand out to others.

TZU SSU.   *The Doctrine of the Mean*, 13.

11. What a man dislikes in those above him, he must not bring to bear on those beneath him. What he dislikes in those beneath him, he must not bring to the service of those above him. . . . The treatment which he dislikes from his neighbours on the right, he must not give to those on the left. The treatment which he dislikes from his neighbours on the left, he must not give to those on the right. This is what is meant by the Way of the Measuring Square.

The Great Learning, x, 2 (*Chinese*).

12. Regard your neighbour's gain as your own gain, and regard your neighbour's loss as your own loss.

Kan Yien Phien, 3.

13. Hurt not others with that which pains yourself.

THE BUDDHA.   *Udana*, v, 18.

14. In happiness and suffering, in joy and grief, we should regard all creatures as we regard our own self, and should therefore refrain from inflicting upon others such injury as would appear undesirable to us if inflicted upon ourselves.

Yogashastra, ii, 20 (*Jainism*).

15. Treat others as thou wouldest be treated thyself.

Angad, ii, 29 (*Sikhism*).

16. This is the sum of duty: do naught to others which, if done to thee, would cause thee pain.

Mahabharata, v, 1517.

6

Treating Others Generously

1. It is more blessed to give than to receive.

JESUS, *quoted by* PAUL.   *Acts* xx, 35.

2. Let him give, not grudgingly, or of necessity: for God loveth a cheerful giver.

PAUL.   *2 Corinthians* ix, 7.

3. Bear with the foolish gladly, being wise yourselves.

PAUL.   *2 Corinthians* xi, 19 (R.*V*.).

4. Every man shall give as he is able.

Deuteronomy xvi, 17.

5. This shall be thy knowledge of law: . . . to give to each one that which thou owest, and even beyond that, as much as thou canst.

KOMENSKY.   *The Labyrinth*, xxxix, 7.

6. Show thou kindness to people of humble condition. Show thyself friendly to the man for whom thou hast antipathy.

The Teaching of Amen-em-apt, 195 and 495.

7. He who reckons in goodness does not need to use a tally.

LAO TSE.   *Tao Teh King*, xxvii.

8. To love and benefit another is to have him follow on and love and benefit you. To hate and injure another is to have him follow on and hate and injure you.

Mo Tse, xv.

9. A wise man rejoices in liberality.

Dhammapada, 177.

10. He who gives unto the beggar who comes to him in want . . . makes a friend of him in future troubles.

Rig Veda, x, 117, 3.

11. Let him always practise, according to his ability, with a cheerful heart, the duty of liberality.

Laws of Manu, iv, 227.

12. That gift is good, which is given, at a due time and place, to a meet recipient who can do no service in return.

KRISHNA. *Bhagavad-Gita*, xvii, 20.

7

Returning Good for Ill

1. But I say unto you which hear, Love your enemies, do good to them which hate you.

JESUS.   *Luke* vi, 27.

2. Render to no man evil for evil.

PAUL.   *Romans* xii, 17 (R.*V*.).

3. If thine enemy be hungry, give him bread to eat; and if he be thirsty, give him water to drink: for thou shalt heap coals of fire upon his head.

Proverbs xxv, 21.

4. There are three kinds of men: man in man, who does good for good and evil for evil; man in God, who does good for evil; and man in the devil, who does evil for good.

Welsh Triad.

5. If that which is false be spoken, be gentle.

Golden Verses of the Pythagoreans, 23.

6. It is not right, therefore, to return an injury, or to do evil to any man, however one may have suffered from him.

PLATO.   *Crito*, x.

7. Thou shalt not inflict an injury on him that has attacked thee, when thou art able to return an answer to him on thine own behalf.

The Teaching of Amen-em-apt, 66.

8. To those who are good to me, I am good; to those who are not good to me, I am good also. Thus all get to be good.

LAO TSE. *Tao Teh King*, xlix.

9. The strong man of the South ... takes no revenge for being treated vilely.

TZU SSU. *The Doctrine of the Mean*, 10.

10. When men speak evil of ye, thus must ye train yourselves: Our heart shall be unwavering, no evil word will we send forth, but compassionate of others' welfare will we abide, of kindly heart without resentment.

THE BUDDHA. *Majjhima-Nikaya*, i, 128.

11. Never does hatred cease by hating; hatred ceases by love. Let a man overcome anger by love; let him overcome evil by good.

Dhammapada, 5 and 223.

12. Subdue wrath by forgiveness, conquer vanity by humbleness, fraud by straightforwardness, and vanquish greed through contentment.

Dasha-vaikalika-Sutra, viii, 39 (*Jainism*).

13. Do good for evil, clothe not thy heart with anger.

Farid, vi, 406 (*Sikhism*).

14. Against an angry man let him not in return show anger, let him bless when he is cursed.

Laws of Manu, vi, 48.

15. Unto friends and unto foes alike in tolerance.

KRISHNA. *Bhagavad-Gita*, xiv, 25.

The Law of Reincarnation

8

Conditions of Life are the Results of Past Lives

1. Who did sin, this man, or his parents, that he was born blind?

John ix, 2.

2. Being good, I came into a body undefiled.

Wisdom of Solomon viii, 20.

3. All pure spirits who are in conformity with the divine dispensation . . . in the course of time they are sent down to inhabit sinless bodies; but the souls of those who have committed self-destruction are doomed to a region in the darkness of the underworld.

JOSEPHUS.   *Wars of the Jews*, iii, 8, 5.

4. [The Judge] sealeth that soul . . . and will have it cast into a body which is suitable to the sins which it hath committed.

Pistis Sophia (p. 261 *b, Coptic MS.*).

5. Is it not rational that souls should be introduced into bodies, in accordance with their merits and previous deeds, and that those who have used their bodies in doing the utmost possible good should have a right to bodies endowed with qualities superior to the bodies of others?

ORIGEN.   *Contra Celsum*, i, 32.

6. Know that if you become worse you will go to the worse souls, or if better to the better, and in every succession of life and death you will do and suffer what like may fitly suffer at the hands of like.

PLATO. *Laws,* x.

7. That there is reincarnation may be plainly seen by the blemishes men have from their birth. Why else are some born blind, and others paralytic, and others diseased in the soul itself?

SALLUSTIUS. *De Diis et Mundo.*

8. The gods . . . allot to each individual his appropriate destiny, one that is in harmony with his past conduct, in conformity with his successive existences.

Such things as happen to the good without justice, as punishments, or poverty, or disease, may be said to take place through offences committed in a former life.

PLOTINUS. *Enneads,* ii, 9, 9; iv, 3, 16.

9. The souls . . . are born again, and divine Justice gives them a new body, in accordance with their merits and demerits.

PORPHYRY. *Concerning Abstinence.*

10. Those who, in the season of prosperity, experience pain and grief, suffer them on account of their words or deeds in a former body, for which the Most Just now punisheth them.

The Desatir (*Zoroastrianism*).

11. Of deeds done and accumulated with deliberate intent I declare there is no wiping out. That wiping out has to come to pass either in this very life or in some

other life at its proper occasion. Without experiencing the result of deeds so done, I declare there is no making an end of ill.

THE BUDDHA. *Anguttara-Nikaya*, v. 292.

12. To have done good deeds in a former existence . . . this is a supreme blessing.

Sutta-Nipata, ii, 4, 3.

13. Karma is the root of birth and death.

Uttaradhyayana-Sutra, xxxii, 7 (*Jainism*).

14. Hence they say that a man is born into the world which he has made.

Satapatha Brahmana, vi, 2, 2, 27.

15. According unto his deeds the embodied one successively assumes forms in various conditions.

Svetasvatara Upanishad, v, 11.

16. With whatever disposition of mind a man performs any act, he reaps its result in a future body endowed with the same quality.

Laws of Manu, xii, 81.

17. The work of Brahmans, Kshatriyas, Vaisyas and Sudras [the four castes] is fixed by reason of the Qualities planted in each.

KRISHNA. *Bhagavad-Gita*, xviii, 41.

18. Our deeds still travel with us from afar,
    And what we have been makes us what we are.

GEORGE ELIOT.

9

Reincarnation

1. And if ye will receive it, this is Elias.

JESUS.   Matthew xi, 14.

2. Whom do men say that I the Son of man am? And they said, Some say that thou art John the Baptist; some Elias; and others, Jeremias, or one of the prophets.

JESUS.   Matthew xvi, 13–14.

3. But I say unto you, That Elias is come already. . . . Then the disciples understood that he spake unto them of John the Baptist.

JESUS.   Matthew xvii, 12–13.

4. The first man Adam was made a living soul; the last Adam was made a quickening spirit.

PAUL.   1 Corinthians xv, 45.

5. The world of iniquity among our members is the tongue, which defileth the whole body, and setteth on fire the wheel of birth.

James iii, 6 (R.V.).

6. Him that overcometh will I make a pillar in the temple of my God, and he shall go no more out.

Revelation iii, 12.

7. Thou turnest man to destruction; and sayest, Return, ye children of men.

Psalm xc, 3.

8. All souls are subjected to the tests of transmigration. ... Souls must in the end be plunged back into the substance from which they came. But before this happens, they must have developed all the perfections the germs of which are implanted within them.

The Zohar.

9. Three necessities of Transmigration: the least of all things, whence a beginning; the substance of all things, whence progress; and the formation of all things, whence individuality.

Welsh Triad.

10. I have been in many shapes before I attained a congenial form.

TALIESIN (*Welsh Bard*).

11. From you [the Britons] we learn that the destination of man's spirit is not the grave; nor the kingdom of the shades. The same spirit animates another body, and if your teaching be true, death is but the centre, not the finish, of a long journey.

LUCAN. *Pharsalia*, i, 509–515.

12. Among them [the Druids] the doctrine of Pythagoras had force, namely, that the souls of men are undying, and that after a fixed number of years they begin to live again, the soul passing into another body.

DIODORUS OF SICILY.

13. As one of their leading dogmas they [the Druids] inculcate this: that souls are not annihilated, but pass after death from one body to another.

CAESAR.   *De Bello Gallico*, vi, 14.

14. The mistakes and sufferings of human life make me think sometimes that these ancient seers ... had some glimpses of the truth, when they said that men are born in order to suffer the penalty for some sins committed in a former life.

CICERO.   *Treatise on Glory.*

15. They will not discharge that soul from the changes of the body until it hath yielded its last circuit according to its merit.

Pistis Sophia (p. 261 *b, Coptic MS.*).

16. In that [mortal] region, Desire and Necessity will be your masters. ... Howbeit, not at random have I ordained the changes of your state; but as your condition will be changed for the worse if you do aught unseemly, so it will be changed for the better if you resolve on action worthy of your origin.

HERMES TRISMEGISTUS.

17. Every one of those who descend to earth is, according to his deserts, or agreeably to the position which he occupied there, ordained to be born in this world, in a different country, or among a different nation, or in a different mode of life, or surrounded by infirmities of a different kind, or to be descended from religious parents, or parents who are not religious.

ORIGEN.   *De Principiis*, 4, i, 23.

18. Pythagoras was reported to have been the first of the Greeks to teach the doctrine that the soul, passing through the circle of necessity, was various times to various living bodies.

DIOGENES LAERTIUS. *Life of Pythagoras.*

19. Souls departing hence exist there, and return hither again.

PLATO. *Phaedo* (70).

20. Thus saith the maiden Lachesis, the daughter of Necessity. Ye short-lived souls, a new generation of men shall here begin the cycle of its mortal existence. Your destiny shall not be allotted to you, but you shall choose it for yourselves. . . . The experience of their former life generally guided the choice.

PLATO. *The Republic*, x, 15.

21. The father Jupiter, commiserating laborious souls, made the bonds about which they labour mortal, causing them to have periodical cessations of their toil, and a liberation from body.

PLOTINUS. *Ennead*, iv, 3, 12.

22. I have entered in as a man of no understanding, and I shall come forth in the form of a strong Spirit.

The Egyptian Book of the Dead, lxiv B, 22.

23. He who fails in attaining Tao, in his highest attainment will see the light, but will descend and be of the earth.

Kwang Tse, xi, 4.

24. Though men may stand to each other in the relation of ruler and minister, that is but for a time. In a changed age, the one of them would not be able to look down on the other.

Kwang Tse, xxvi, 8.

25. Many a birth have I traversed in this round of lives and deaths, vainly seeking the builder of the house.

Dhammapada, 153.

26. As a wayfarer takes a brief lodging, so he that is travelling through the way of existence finds in each birth but a passing rest.

Bodhicharyavatara (Buddhism).

27. When the time for his rebirth arrives . . . then Time unites him again with activities selected from the accumulation of past activities.

Devi Bhagavata.

28. Entering into the state of existence the living being builds its own appropriate body; being embodied he gets the senses. Through the senses, objects in the environment are perceived; from perception comes desire or aversion towards those objects; and from desire the cycle begins again.

Panchastikaya-sara, 136 *(Jainism).*

29. Naked didst thou come, naked shalt thou go; thou shalt become a morsel for death, and return to a body again and again.

Arjan, iii, 152 *(Sikhism).*

30. When one's mind is attached . . . he comes again from that world to this world because of his action.

Brihad-aranyaka Upanishad, iv, 4, 6.

31. Like a grain a mortal ripens. Like a grain he is born hither again.

Katha Upanishad, i, 6.

32. Let him reflect on the transmigrations of men . . . on the departure of the individual soul from this body and its new birth in another womb, and on its wanderings through ten thousand millions of existences.

Laws of Manu, vi, 61–63.

33. As a man casts off worn-out clothes, and puts on other new clothes, so the spirit casts off worn-out bodies, and puts on other new bodies.

KRISHNA.   *Bhagavad-Gita*, ii, 22.

34. They will come back—come back again, as long as
        the red Earth rolls.
    He never wasted a leaf or a tree.   Do you think He
        would squander souls?

RUDYARD KIPLING.   *The Sack of the Gods.*

35. I hold that when a person dies
        His soul returns again to earth;
    Arrayed in some new flesh-disguise,
        Another mother gives him birth.
    With sturdier limbs and brighter brain
        The old soul takes the road again.

JOHN MASEFIELD.   *A Creed.*

10

The Allotted Span of Life

1. Is there not an appointed time to man upon earth? His days are determined, the number of his months is with thee, and thou has appointed his bounds that he cannot pass.

Job vii, 1; xiv, 5.

2. Behold, thou hast made my days as an handbreadth.

Psalm xxxix, 5.

3. He gave them days by number, and a set time.

Ecclesiasticus xvii, 2 (R.*V.*).

4. The law . . . is to enter mortal bodies and after certain prescribed periods be again set free.

PHILO OF ALEXANDRIA.

5. On the day in which the Rulers breathed the power into the body, they sealed . . . also the number of years which the soul will spend in the body.

Pistis Sophia (p. 231 *a*, *Coptic MS.*).

6. Nor has my approaching end happened by mere chance.

PLATO. *Apology of Socrates*, xxxiii.

7. Thou art an actor in a play, of such a part as it may please the director to assign thee; of a short part if he choose a short part, of a long part if he choose a long part.

EPICTETUS.   *Encheiridon*, xvii.

8. There is but a certain limit of time appointed unto thee.

MARCUS AURELIUS.   *Meditations*, ii, 1.

9. Through fate he then departs.

The Avesta, Vendidad, v, 8.

10. A man lives his allotted hour of life.

The Teaching of Amen-em-apt, 487.

11. The death of man has its appointed time.

Kwang Tse, xxix, 3.

12. The Master came, because it was his time to be born; he went, because it was his time to die.

Kwang Tse, iii, 4.

13. When their term of life is exhausted they die.

Kan Ying Phien, 2.

14. Let not my thread . . . be severed, nor my work's sum be shattered before the time.

Rig Veda, ii, 28, 5.

11

Death is Not to be Feared or Mourned

1. I would not have you to be ignorant, brethren, concerning them which are asleep, that ye sorrow not, even as others which have no hope.

PAUL.   1 Thessalonians iv, 13.

2. The day of death is better than the day of one's birth.

Ecclesiastes vii, 1.

3. In the sight of the unwise they seemed to die: and their departure is taken for misery, and their going from us to be utter destruction: but they are in peace.

Wisdom of Solomon iii, 2–3.

4. They do mourn and lament no man's death, unless it be one whom they see depart from his life full of care, and against his will.

SIR THOMAS MORE.   Utopia, Book II.

5. The fact is that so far from mourning death you ought to honour it and reverence it.

APOLLONIUS OF TYANA.   To Valerius.

6. Those would I teach, and by right reason bring to think of death as but an idle thing. Why thus affrighted by an empty name? . . . nor dies the spirit, but new life repeats in other forms, and only changes seats.

PYTHAGORAS.   OVID, Metamorphoses.

7. It comes together and is dispersed and goes back whence it came; earth to earth, and the breath on high. What hardship is in that? None.

EPICHARMUS.

8. Death is one or other of two things: either it is such that the dead man is annihilated . . . when death would be an extraordinary gain. . . . But if, on the contrary, death be a sort of travelling from hence to another place, and what is reported to be true, that all the dead are there, what greater blessing can there be than this?

PLATO.   *Apology of Socrates*, xxxii.

9. Death is a cessation from the impression of the senses, the tyranny of the passions, the error of the mind, and the servitude of the body.

MARCUS AURELIUS.   *Meditations*, vi, 26.

10. A stone I died and rose again a plant,
   A plant I died and rose an animal;
   I died an animal and was born a man.
   Why should I fear? What have I lost by death?

JALALU'D-DIN RUMI.

11. If the people do not fear death, how then can you frighten them by death?

LAO TSE.   *Tao Teh King*, lxxiv.

12. The ancients spoke of the dead as "men who have returned."

LIEH TSE.

13. Look on death as going home.

Kwang Tse, xvii, 9.

14. The world is afflicted with death and decay, therefore the wise do not grieve, knowing the terms of the world.

Sutta-Nipata, iii, 8, 8.

15. During this time [after death] no relative or fond mate should be allowed to weep or wail, as such is not good; so restrain them.

The Tibetan Book of the Dead, i, 1.

16. One who identifies himself with his soul regards bodily transmigration of his soul at death fearlessly, like changing one cloth for another.

Samadhi Shataka, 77 (*Jainism*).

17. This person, by being born and obtaining a body, is joined with evils. When he departs, on dying, he leaves evils behind.

Brihad-aranyaka Upanishad, iv, 3, 8.

18. In the final hour one should take refuge in these three thoughts: "You are the Indestructible; you are the Unshaken; you are the very essence of life."

Chandogya Upanishad, iii, 17, 6.

19. Certain is death for the born, and certain is birth for the dead: therefore what is inevitable ought not to be a cause of thy sorrow.

KRISHNA. *Bhagavad-Gita*, ii, 27.

20. We are the ghosts of the departed,
    Souls of those who once were with you . . .
    Cries of grief and lamentation . . .
    Cries of anguish from the living . . .
    Sadden us with useless sorrow.

Hiawatha, xix.

Death is Not an End

1. God is not the God of the dead, but of the living.

JESUS.   *Matthew* xxii, 32.

2. That which thou sowest is not quickened, except it die.

PAUL.   1 *Corinthians* xv, 36.

3. Or ever the silver cord be loosed, or the golden bowl be broken, or the pitcher be broken at the fountain, or the wheel broken at the cistern. Then shall the dust return to the earth as it was: and the spirit shall return unto God who gave it.

Ecclesiastes xii, 6.

4. When the body dies . . . The astral soul comes from the astral plane and returns to it. The body comes from Nature and returns to it. Thus everything returns to its own *prima materia.*

PARACELSUS.   *De Morbis Invis.*, iv.

5. The change from being to becoming seems to be birth, and the change from becoming to being seems to be death, but in reality no one is ever born, nor does one ever die.

APOLLONIUS OF TYANA.   *To Valerius.*

6. [The doctrine of the Essenes is] that souls . . . are united to their bodies as in prisons, . . . but that when

they are set free from the bonds of the flesh, they then, as
released from a long bondage, rejoice and mount upward.

JOSEPHUS.   *Wars of the Jews*, ii, 8, 11.

7. . . . and each part return thither whence it came into
the light of day—the breath into the air of heaven, the
body into earth. For the body is not ours in fee; we are
but lifelong tenants.

EURIPIDES.

8. . . . the soul separated from the body and existing apart
by itself. Is death anything else but this? Nothing else.

PLATO.   *Phaedo* (64).

9. The door is opened . . . to the place from which thou
camest—to things friendly and akin to thee, to the
elements of Being. Whatever in thee was of fire, shall go
to fire; of earth, to earth; of air, to air; of water, to water.

EPICTETUS.   *Dissertations*, iii, 13.

10. It is necessary that the soul should fly from an
association with the body, and a separation from the body
is a flight from generation to real essence.

PLOTINUS.   *Ennead*, ii, 9, 6.

11. As the stalks grow with the corn, yet, when they come
to maturity, these are cast away, thus too the body which
is fastened to the soul at birth is not a part of the man.

PORPHYRY.   *Letter to Marcella*, xxxii.

12. There comes a day . . . when the soul leaves that body
full of desires; but his virtue, which is of all existences the
greatest, the best, the finest, never parts from a man.

Aogemadaccha, 52 (Zoroastrianism).

13. Thine essence is in heaven, thy body is in the earth.

Pyramid of Teta, line 304.

14. It is the cutting off of the corruptible in the body of Osiris, the scribe Ani, victorious before all the gods.

The Egyptian Book of the Dead, xvii, 40.

15. Life and death are simply a going forth and a coming back. . . . Things that have been endowed with life die; but that which produces life itself never comes to an end.

Lieh Tse, i.

16. Birth is not a beginning; death is not an end.

Kwang Tse, xxiii, 9.

17. The ancients described death as the loosening of the cord on which the Lord suspended the life. What we can point to are the faggots that have been consumed; but the fire is transmitted elsewhere.

Kwang Tse, iii, 4.

18. Naught else but Ill it is doth pass away.

Samyutta-Nikaya, iv.

19. Verily, indeed, when life has left it, this body dies. The life does not die.

Chandogya Upanishad, vi, 11, 3.

20. Death hath not touched it [the spirit] at all, dead though the house of it seems!

KRISHNA. *Bhagavad-Gita*, ii, 20.

The Composition of Man

1 3

Body, Soul and Spirit

1. Fear not them which kill the body, but are not able to kill the soul.

JESUS.   *Matthew* x, 28.

2. May your spirit and soul and body be preserved.

PAUL. 1 *Thessalonians* v, 23 (R.*V*.).

3. . . . piercing even to the dividing asunder of soul and spirit.

PAUL. *Hebrews* iv, 12.

4. The body without the spirit is dead.

James ii, 26.

5. The Lord God formed man of the dust of the ground, and breathed into his nostrils the breath of life; and man became a living soul.

Genesis ii, 7.

6. . . . that moulded him, and . . . inspired into him an active soul, and breathed into him a vital spirit.

Wisdom of Solomon xv, 11.

7. As to the situation of Mansoul, it lieth just between the two worlds.

JOHN BUNYAN. *The Holy War*.

8. We claim that this world of external appearances is only the fourth part of the actual world.

PARACELSUS. *De Generatio Hominis.*

9. Man is composed of indestructible and metaphysical substance, as well as of material and destructible substance, but in such a manner that the indestructible and eternal is, as it were, imprisoned in the destructible matter.

ECKARTSHAUSEN. *The Cloud upon the Sanctuary,* iv.

10. God made man from the dust and inserted a soul and a spirit.

JOSEPHUS. 1 *Antiquities,* i, 2.

11. The man and his body are different things. . . . What, therefore, is the man? . . . He is that which uses his body.

PLATO. *The First Alcibiades.*

12. The soul when in the body is the source of life, and gives the power of breath and revival, and when this reviving power fails then the body perishes and dies . . . and the body is an enclosure or prison in which the soul is incarcerated . . . until the penalty is paid.

PLATO. *Cratylus* (399–400).

13. The body, the soul, the understanding. As the senses naturally belong to the body, and the desires and affections to the soul, so do the principles to the understanding.

MARCUS AURELIUS. *Meditations,* iii, 16.

14. With respect to our soul, one part of it always abides on high, another part of it is conversant with sensibles, and another has a subsistence in the middle of these.

PLOTINUS. *Ennead*, ii, 9, 2.

15. When the prescribed period arrives, souls may as it were spontaneously descend, and enter into that receptacle in which it is necessary for them to reside.

PLOTINUS. *Ennead*, iv, 3, 12.

16. Only by communication in Soul is body moved from within. . . . Soul must be ranked below the unmoved Principle whose unmoved existence is its activity.

PROCLUS. *Elements of Theology*, 20.

17. The Father of men and gods placed Mind in Soul, and Soul in inert Body.

Chaldean Oracles (Kroll 47).

18. My spirit shall be as an amulet for my body and as one that watcheth [to protect] my soul.

The Egyptian Book of the Dead, lxiv, 49.

19. The self-controlled man regards his body as outside of himself.

LAO TSE. *Tao Teh King*, vii.

20. The Town is this body. . . . The Six Gates thereof are the avenues of Sense. . . . The Lord of the Town is the Mind.

THE BUDDHA. *Sutta-Nipata*, iv, 194.

21. All creatures are one fourth of him, three fourths eternal life in heaven. With three fourths Purusha went up: one fourth of him again was here.

Rig Veda, x, 90, 3.

22. Know thou the self as riding in a chariot, and the body as that chariot. Know thou the will as the charioteer, and the mind as the reins. The senses, they say, are the horses, and the objects of sense are the road.

Katha Upanishad, iii, 3.

23. He who sees with the eye, and he who moves in dreams, he who is deep asleep, and he who is beyond the deep sleeper—these are a person's four distinct conditions. . . . In the three a quarter Brahma moves; a three-quarter in the last.

Maitri Upanishad, vii, 11 (7).

24. That which impels the body to action, the wise call "the knower of the field"; and that body which thence derives active functions, they name "composed of elements." Another internal, called "the individual soul," attends the birth of all creatures embodied, and thence in all mortal forms is conveyed perception.

Laws of Manu, xii, 12–13.

25. When, in this world of manifested life, the undying Spirit, setting forth from Me, taketh on form, it draweth to itself . . . senses and intellect.

KRISHNA. *Bhagavad-Gita*, xv, 7.

26. Strong are the senses; stronger than the senses is the mind; stronger than the mind is the understanding; but stronger than the understanding is the Spirit.

KRISHNA. *Bhagavad-Gita*, iii, 42.

14

Soul: the Vehicle of Thought
and Feeling

1. My soul is exceeding sorrowful.

JESUS. *Matthew* xxvi, 38.

2. Three grand powers of the soul: affection, understanding and will.

Welsh Triad.

3. The principal powers of the soul are three—to live, to
feel, and to reason.... By "mind" we mean the highest
and noblest part of the soul.

DANTE. *The Banquet,* iii, 2, 3–4.

4. The three inner parts of man, his intellect, his will,
and his affections.

KOMENSKY. *The Way of Light,* viii, 7.

5. Soul is defined as a substance of understanding and
feeling.

ORIGEN. *De Principiis,* 2, viii, 1.

6. We call that with which one reasons the rational part
of the soul, but that part with which it loves, and
hungers, and thirsts, and is carried away by desires, the
irrational and concupiscent part ... there is likewise in
the soul also a third element of spiritedness.

PLATO. *The Republic,* iv, 15–16.

7. Pain . . . either is in regard of the body (and that cannot be, because the body of itself is altogether insensible): or in regard of the soul.

MARCUS AURELIUS. *Meditations*, viii, 26.

8. Reasoning is the active operation of a soul.

PLOTINUS. *Ennead*, i, 1, 7.

9. Inasmuch as body is not the self . . . it is impermanent. . . . So also is it with feeling, perception, the activities and sense-consciousness.

THE BUDDHA. *Vinaya-Pitaka*, i, 6.

15

Healing

1. Say in a word, and my servant shall be healed.

Luke vii, 7.

2. There was not found a healing for their life, because they were worthy to be punished.

Wisdom of Solomon xvi, 9 (R.*V*.).

3. Of the most High cometh healing.

Ecclesiasticus xxxviii, 2.

4. Pythagoras said that the most divine art was that of healing. And if the healing art is most divine, it must occupy itself with the soul as well as with the body; for no creature can be sound so long as the higher part of it is sickly.

APOLLONIUS OF TYANA.   *To Criton.*

5. The physician should know the invisible as well as the visible man. . . . There is a great difference between the power which removes the invisible cause of disease, and which is Magic, and that which causes merely external effects to disappear.

PARACELSUS.   *Paragranum.*

6. It is most necessary that the physician should have control of essentials.

HIPPOCRATES.

7. As you ought not to attempt to cure the eyes without the head, or the head without the body, so neither ought you to attempt to cure the body without the soul.

PLATO. *Charmides* (156).

8. If several healers offer themselves ... namely, one who heals with the knife, one who heals with herbs, and one who heals with the holy word, it is this one who will best drive away sickness from the body of the faithful.

The Avesta, Vendidad, vii, 44.

9. The physician must know what it is that gives rise to disease. Only so can he attack it. If he does not know this then he cannot attack it.

Mo Tse, xiv.

16

Sleep and Dreams

1. If there be a prophet among you, I the Lord will make myself known unto him in a vision, and will speak unto him in a dream.

Numbers xii, 6.

2. In a dream, in a vision of the night, when deep sleep falleth upon men, in slumberings upon the bed; then he openeth the ears of men, and sealeth their instruction.

Job xxxiii, 15–16.

3. He giveth to his beloved during sleep.

Psalm cxxvii, 2 (*Luther's Translation*).

4. The Highest gave understanding unto the five men, and they wrote the wonderful visions of the night that were told.

2 Esdras xiv, 42.

5. In the time of rest upon his bed his night sleep doth change his knowledge.

Ecclesiasticus xl, 5 (R.*V.*).

6. I laid me down in my bed, so that perchance my good angel by divine permission might appear, and (as it had formerly happened) instruct me in this affair.

The Marriage of Christian Rosencreutz.

7. There are two gates of Sleep: of horn, fame tells, the one, through which the spirits of truth find an easy passage; the other, wrought smooth—gleaming with sheen of ivory, but false the visions that the nether powers speed therefrom to the heaven above.

VIRGIL.

8. The rest of mankind know not what they are doing when awake, just as they forget what they do in sleep.

HERACLITUS.

9. But all men do not easily recall the things of the other world. . . . Few there are who retain the remembrance of them sufficiently.

PLATO. *Phaedrus* (250).

10. We all work. . . . As I think Heraclitus in a place speaketh of them that sleep, that even they do work in their kind, and do confer to the general operations of the world.

MARCUS AURELIUS. *Meditations*, vi, 37.

11. The Gods themselves . . . are well content, in all manner of ways, as by dreams and oracles, to help.

MARCUS AURELIUS. *Meditations*, ix, 25.

12. Divinity has produced many gods, all of whom are suspended from, and subsist through and by him, and . . . who prophetically announce to men what they there behold, and by oracles unfold their will.

Plotinus, ii, 9, 9.

13. Every night Thou freest our spirits from the body.

JALALU'D-DIN RUMI. *Masnavi.*

14. When we sleep, soul communicates with soul.

Kwang Tse, ii, 2.

15. Upon becoming asleep he transcends this world and the forms of death.

Brihad-aranyaka Upanishad, iv, 3, 7.

16. When a person here sleeps ... he has gone to his own.

Chandogya Upanishad, vi, 8, 1.

Spirit

1. It is the spirit that quickeneth; the flesh profiteth nothing.

JESUS.   *John* vi, 63.

2. God created man to be immortal, and made him to be an image of his own eternity.

Wisdom of Solomon ii, 23.

3. Spirit is a substance, an essence, an absolute reality. Hence its properties are indestructibility, uniformity, penetration, indivisibility and continuity. Matter is not a substance, it is an aggregate. Hence it is destructible, divisible and subject to change.

ECKARTSHAUSEN.   *The Cloud upon the Sanctuary,* iv.

4. From the very beginning have ye been immortal and children of life.

VALENTINUS.   *A Homily.*

5. Every soul is immortal—for whatever is in perpetual motion is immortal ... and that which is self-moved is the beginning of motion, and as such can neither be created nor destroyed.

PLATO.   *Phaedrus* (245).

6. Those who conceive according to the spirit ... bear the things of the spirit ... wisdom and all her sister virtues.

PLATO.   *The Symposium* (209).

7. Nothing that the Will willeth not can hinder or hurt the Will, but itself only can hurt itself.

EPICTETUS. *Dissertations*, iii, 19.

8. Surely nothing that is Real will perish. In the world Yonder the several intelligences will never be lost in unity, for all that they are not divided corporeally; each endures, preserving its proper being in individual difference.

PLOTINUS. *Ennead*, iv, 3, 5.

9. . . . the grand reality of the ever-during Thing.

Kwang Tse, vi, 6.

10. The name of the human spirit is "The Divinity in man."

Kwang Tse, xv, 3.

11. All life is inviolable.

Anguttara-Nikaya, Tetrads, 176.

12. Thine own consciousness, shining, void, and inseparable from the Great Body of Radiance, hath no birth nor death.

The Tibetan Book of the Dead, i, 1.

13. That which is the finest essence—this whole world has that as its soul. That is reality. That is Atman. That art thou.

Chandogya Upanishad, vi, 9, 4.

14. Never the spirit was born; the spirit shall cease to be never.

KRISHNA. *Bhagavad-Gita*, ii, 20.

15. Weapons reach not the Life; flame burns it not, waters cannot o'erwhelm, nor dry winds wither it. Impenetrable, unentered, unassailed, unharmed, untouched, immortal, all-arriving, stable, sure, invisible, ineffable, by word and thought uncompassed, ever all itself.

KRISHNA.   *Bhagavad-Gita*, ii, 23.

Knowledge and Truth

18

The Limitations of Earth-Knowledge

1. The Spirit of truth; whom the world cannot receive, because it seeth him not, neither knoweth him.

JESUS.   *John* xiv, 17.

2. For now we see through a glass, darkly; but then face to face.

PAUL.   1 *Corinthians* xiii, 12.

3. Are not all your ideas borrowed from your senses, which do not give you the reality but only its phenomena? ... For absolute truth is not to be found in the phenomenal world.

ECKARTSHAUSEN.   *The Cloud upon the Sanctuary*, i.

4. Through the medium of dull dim instruments, it is but seldom and with difficulty that people are enabled on meeting with the copies to recognize the character of the original.

PLATO.   *Phaedrus* (250).

5. What really is, may be really known; but what does not exist at all, cannot be known at all. ... It is impossible that what is known and what is matter of opinion should be the same. ... Opinion then is neither knowledge nor is it ignorance ... it lies between the two.

PLATO.   *The Republic*, v, 20–21.

6. In taking knowledge of an object, the soul suffers defect of unity, and is not wholly one; for knowledge is an account of things, and an account is manifold, and so our soul lapses into number and multiplicity, and misses the One.

PLOTINUS. *Ennead,* vi, 9, 4.

7. It would be better to have no books than to believe everything in books.

Mencius, xiv, 3.

8. The Self cannot be gained by knowledge.

Katha Upanishad, i, 2, 23.

19

The Impossibility of Conceiving the Absolute

1. No man hath seen God at any time.

John i, 18.

2. Canst thou by searching find out God? Canst thou find out the Almighty unto perfection?

Job xi, 7.

3. To whom then will ye liken God? or what likeness will ye compare unto him?

Isaiah xl, 18.

4. He is not to be comprehended of any; who can neither be defined by any means, nor conceived by the mind.

The Shepherd of Hermas, Commands, i, 2–3.

5. There are three things that are unknowable: God, Nothing and Infinity.

Welsh Triad.

6. The eternal light is a glory which cannot be approached by the human senses.

KOMENSKY. *The Way of Light*, viii, 5.

7. That which is really ineffable is not named Ineffable, but is superior to every name that is used.

BASILIDES.

8. According to strict truth, God is incomprehensible, and incapable of being measured. . . . God, whose nature cannot be grasped or seen by the power of any human understanding.

ORIGEN. *De Principiis*, i, 1, 5.

9. Of that region beyond the sky no earthly bard has ever yet sung, or ever will sing, in worthy strains.

PLATO. *Phaedrus* (247).

10. It [the One] is in reality ineffable . . . of that which is beyond all things, it is alone true to assert that it has not any other name [than "ineffable"]. . . . Properly speaking, however, there is no name of it, because nothing can be asserted of it.

PLOTINUS. *Ennead*, v, 3, 13.

11. Tao that can be expressed in words is not eternal and unchanging Tao.

LAO TSE. *Tao Teh King*, i.

12. Great Tao cannot be talked about.

Kwang Tse, ii, 7.

13. With what is limited to pursue after what is un-limited is a perilous thing.

Kwang Tse, iii, 1.

14. Measure not with words the Immeasurable; nor sink the string of thought into the Fathomless.

THE BUDDHA. *The Light of Asia*, viii.

15. Were the earth to become paper, the forest pens, and the wind a writer, the end of the endless one could not be described.

Arjan, iii, 323 (*Sikhism*).

16. His voice is heard, his shape is ever viewless.

Rig Veda, x, 168, 4.

17. Not by sight is It grasped, not even by speech, not by any other sense-organs, austerity, or work.

Mundaka Upanishad, iii, 1, 8.

18. Sustainer of all, of form inconceivable.

KRISHNA. *Bhagavad-Gita*, viii, 9.

19. Para-Brahm, which cannot be called either being or non-being.

KRISHNA. *Bhagavad-Gita*, xiii, 12.

20

Faith, based on Knowledge

1. Faith cometh by hearing, and hearing by the word of Christ.

PAUL.   *Romans* x, 17.

2. He who wants to obtain true faith must know, because faith grows out of spiritual knowledge. The faith that comes from that knowledge is rooted in the heart.

PARACELSUS.   *De Fundamento Sapientae.*

3. There is at last produced that living faith, by which we find, within ourselves, as something that is true in our own experience, all that we have believed in hitherto merely with the confidence of a child.

ECKARTSHAUSEN.   *The Cloud upon the Sanctuary,* vi.

4. Having faith we must strive with all our might to know.

PORPHYRY.   *Letter to Marcella,* xxiv.

5. Faith is verification by the heart.

Sufi Saying.

6. If I have knowledge and resolute faith I shall walk in the Great Tao.

LAO TSE.   *Tao Teh King,* liii.

7. Without faith where can a man take hold?

Mencius, xii, 12.

8.   He who knows what Man is, rests in the knowledge of the known, waiting for the unknown.

Kwang Tse, vi, 1.

9.   Faith is in this world the best property for a man.

Sutta-Nipata, i, 10, 2.

10. Belief in things ascertained as they are is right belief.

Tattvartha-Sutra, i, 2 (*Jainism*).

11. By faith is Agni kindled.

Taittiriya Brahmana, ii, 8, 8, 6.

12. The faith of each is according to his pre-dispositions.

KRISHNA.   *Bhagavad-Gita*, xvii, 3.

2 1

Proof, by One's Own Experience

1. If any man will do his will, he shall know of the doctrine, whether it be of God, or whether I speak of myself.

JESUS.   *John* vii, 17.

2. [The Samaritans] said unto the woman, Now we believe, not because of thy saying: for we have heard him ourselves and know.

John iv, 42.

3. Prove all things.

PAUL.   1 *Thessalonians* v, 21.

4. Truth is the science of wisdom preserved in memory by conscience.

Book of Dwyfyddiaeth (*Welsh*).

5. For knowledge in effect is to know a thing as it is in itself and not as it is reputed to be.

KOMENSKY.   *The Way of Light*, xiv, 20.

6. Everything proves itself by itself as soon as we have acquired the interior experience of the truths revealed through faith, so soon as we are led by faith to vision, or in other words, to full cognizance.

ECKARTSHAUSEN.   *The Cloud upon the Sanctuary*, iv.

7. Of existing things knowledge alone is permanent, and the truth which is derived from wisdom.

ORIGEN.   *Contra Celsum*, iii, 72.

8. Our knowledge is nothing but reminiscence.

PLATO.   *Phaedo* (72).

9. Cast away from thee opinion, and thou art safe.

MARCUS AURELIUS.   *Meditations*, xii, 19.

10. Consciousness is the sole basis of certainty. . . . Knowledge has three degrees—opinion, science, illumination. The means or instrument of the first is sense; of the second dialectic; of the third intuition.

PLOTINUS.   *Letter to Flaccus.*

11. He who has not tasted does not know.

JALALU'D-DIN RUMI.   *Masnavi.*

12. Only as I know a thing myself, do I know it.

Kwang Tse, ii, 3.

13. When they say to a man who sees with his eyes, "Have you seen?" and he says, "I have seen," that is the truth.

Brihad-aranyaka Upanishad, iv, 1, 4.

14. Only that knowledge knows which knows the known by the knower.

KRISHNA.   *Bhagavad-Gita*, xiii, 2.

22

Truth

---

1. The truth of the Lord endureth for ever.

Psalm cxvii, 2.

2. That which hath been is that which shall be, . . . and there is no new thing under the sun.

Ecclesiastes i, 9.

3. Three things which are one: truth, knowledge, and light.

Welsh Triad.

4. Truth is eternal; if a man neglects it, still it remains.
KOMENSKY. *The Way of Light*, x, 7 (12).

5. The Light is a judge of truth.

Pistis Sophia (p. 161 *b*, *Coptic MS.*).

6. The same thing which is now called Christian religion existed among the ancients, nor was wanting at any time from the beginning of the human race. . . . They now call Christian the true religion which existed before.

ST. AUGUSTINE. *Opera*, i, p. 12.

7. Can you find anything more akin to wisdom than truth?

PLATO. *The Republic*, vi, 2.

8. Real existence, colourless, formless and intangible, visible only to the intelligence which sits at the helm of soul, and with which the family of true science is concerned, has its abode in this region beyond the sky.

PLATO. Phaedrus (247).

9. He who sees what now is, hath seen all that ever hath been from times everlasting, and that shall be to eternity. There is nothing that is new.

MARCUS AURELIUS. Meditations, vi, 34; vii, 1.

10. There can be found no Reality truer than the truth.

PLOTINUS. Ennead, v, 5, 2.

11. There is great power in Truth [Maät] for she is permanent.

The Teaching of Ptah-hotep, v.

12. Truth is one, there is not a second, about which one intelligent man might dispute with another.

Sutta-Nipata, iv, 12, 7.

13. Truth is one: though the wise call it by various names.

Rig Veda, i, 164, 46.

14. Verily, that which is Law is truth.

Brihad-aranyaka Upanishad, i, 4, 14.

15. That which is can never cease to be; that which is not will not exist.

KRISHNA. Bhagavad-Gita, ii, 16.

Ignorance and Error

23

Obscuration

1. Can the blind lead the blind? Shall they not both fall into the ditch?

JESUS.   *Luke* vi, 39.

2. Ye are dull of hearing. For when for the time ye ought to be teachers, ye have need that one teach you again which be the first principles of the oracles of God.

PAUL.   *Hebrews* v, 12.

3. ... but having itching ears, will heap to themselves teachers after their own lusts; and will turn away their ears from the truth, and turn aside unto fables.

2 *Timothy* iv, 3 (R.*V.*).

4. My people hearkened not to my voice; and Israel would none of me. So I let them go after the stubbornness of their heart, that they might walk in their own counsels.

Psalm lxxxi, 11–12 (R.*V.*).

5. Where there is no vision, the people perish.

Proverbs xxix, 18.

6. The vision of all is become unto you as the words of a book that is sealed, which men deliver to one that is learned, saying, Read this, I pray thee: and he saith, I cannot; for it is sealed.

Isaiah xxix, 11.

7. I will send a famine in the land, not a famine of bread, nor a thirst for water, but of hearing the words of the Lord.

Amos viii, 11.

8. But preachers . . . because they saw men unwilling to frame their manners to Christ's rule, have twisted and distorted his doctrine . . . that by some means at least they might agree together.

SIR THOMAS MORE. *Utopia*, Book 1.

9. The laws are made but who is led by law?
   Not one, because the Pastor who precedes,
   The whilst considering has not healed the sore,
   So that the flock who craved a guide no longer heeds.

DANTE. *Purgatorio*, xvi, 22.

10. In politics and religion the world is now full of falsehood and counterfeit: everywhere men accept opinions instead of the truth.

KOMENSKY. *The Way of Light, Dedication*, 25.

11. The brighter the light of Truth which shines on a man, and the more obstinately he resists it, the more complete the blindness which he brings on himself.

KOMENSKY. *The Way of Light*, xi, 11.

12. Mistakes in practical affairs are through the ignorance of the man who thinks he knows when he does not.

PLATO. *The First Alcibiades.*

13. The cause of our utter ignorance of God lies in the price we put upon sensible things, the small account we make of ourselves.

PLOTINUS.   *Ennead*, v, 1, 1.

14. The intoxication of life and its pleasures and occupations veils the Truth from men's eyes.

JALALU'D-DIN RUMI.   *Masnavi.*

15. When virtue is lost, benevolence appears; when benevolence is lost, right conduct appears; when right conduct is lost, expediency appears. Expediency is the mere shadow of right and truth; it is the beginning of disorder.

LAO TSE.   *Tao Teh King*, xxxviii.

16. Tao becomes obscured through the small comprehension.

Kwang Tse, ii, 3.

17. Ignorance is the worst of all stains.

Dhammapada, 243.

18. When one blind man is the guide of another they both lose their way.

Sutra-Kritanga, i, 1, 2, 19 (*Jainism*).

19. Those abiding in the midst of ignorance, self-wise, thinking themselves learned, running hither and thither, go around deluded, like blind men led by one who is himself blind.

Katha Upanishad, ii, 5.

20. Then, with the lapse of years, the truth grew dim and perished. . . . Knowledge is darkened by ignorance, and mankind becomes deluded.

KRISHNA. *Bhagavad-Gita*, iv, 2; v, 15.

21. They remembered no more the Heart of Heaven, and behold how they fell.

The Popol Vuh, i, 2.

22. Outwardly splendid as of old—
   Inwardly sparkless, void and cold—
   Her force and fire all spent and gone—
   Like the dead moon, she still shines on.

SIR WILLIAM WATSON. *The Church To-day.*

24

The Nature of Sin

1. Not that which goeth into the mouth defileth a man; but that which cometh out of the mouth, this defileth a man.

JESUS.   Matthew xv, 11.

2. Every sin that a man doeth is without the body.

PAUL.   1 Corinthians vi, 18.

3. Dead in trespasses and sins; . . . fulfilling the desires of the flesh and of the mind.

PAUL.   Ephesians ii, 1–3.

4. He that sinneth shall offend against his own soul.

Ecclesiasticus xix, 4.

5. Men are liable to sin . . . from the time they are made capable of understanding and knowledge, when the reason implanted within has suggested to them the difference between good and evil; and after they have already begun to know what evil is, they are made liable to sin, if they commit it.

ORIGEN.   De Principiis, 1, iii, 6.

6. Every man is good in that in which he is wise, and bad in that in which he is unwise.

PLATO.   Laches (194).

7. The nature and essence of the Good is in a certain disposition of the Will; likewise that of the Evil.

EPICTETUS. *Dissertations*, i, 29, i.

8. He that sinneth, sinneth unto himself. He that is unjust, hurts himself, in that he makes himself worse than he was before.

MARCUS AURELIUS. *Meditations*, ix, 4.

9. There is no greater sin than indulging desire.

LAO TSE. *Tao Teh King*, xlvi.

10. Anger, intoxication, obstinacy, bigotry, deceit, envy, grandiloquence, pride and conceit, intimacy with the unjust; this is what defiles one, not the eating of flesh.

Sutta-Nipata, ii, 2, 7.

11. Passion and hatred . . . originate in desire.

Sutta-Nipata, ii, 5, 1.

12. Pondering on objects of the sense there springs attraction; from attraction grows desire; from desire is produced passion; from passion comes delusion; from delusion results obscuration of memory.

KRISHNA. *Bhagavad-Gita*, ii, 63.

25

Earth-Riches

1. Lay not up for yourselves treasures upon earth.

JESUS.   *Matthew* vi, 19.

2. They that desire to be rich fall into a temptation and a snare and many foolish and hurtful lusts, such as drown men in destruction and perdition.

1 *Timothy* vi, 9 (R.*V.*).

3. Thou shalt not covet.

Exodus xx, 17.

4. Better is little with the fear of the Lord, than great treasure and trouble therewith. Better is a dinner of herbs where love is, than a stalled ox and hatred therewith.

Proverbs xv, 16–17.

5. According to his riches his anger riseth.

Ecclesiasticus xxviii, 10.

6. He who takes care of his money takes care neither of himself nor of what is his, but of things still further removed from what is his.

PLATO.   *The First Alcibiades.*

7. Thou shouldst not become presumptuous through much treasure and wealth; for in the end it is necessary for thee to leave it all.

Menog-i Khrad, ii, 102 (*Zoroastrianism*).

8. In wealth, fear is concealed and peril is hidden. There is no continuance in the riches of this world; that which is subject to mortality and undergoeth a change, hath never been and is not worth regarding.

BAHA-U-LLAH.

9. Be not covetous towards thy kindred.

The Teaching of Ptah-hotep, xx.

10. Better is the beggar who is in the hand of the Almighty, than the rich who are safely housed in a comfortable dwelling. Better are bread-cakes of flour and water with a loving heart, than rich meats that carry with them bickering and quarrelling.

The Teaching of Amen-em-apt, 158–161.

11. You may be weighted with honours and become proud; misfortune then will come to your Self.

LAO TSE. *Tao Teh King*, ix.

12. For the man of benevolence wealth is the means by which the individual self is expanded. For the man without benevolence the individual is a tool for the expansion of wealth.

The Great Learning, vii (*Chinese*).

13. The foolish by his thirst for riches destroys himself.

Dhammapada, 355.

14. He who covets extensively ... sins will overpower him, dangers will crush him, and pain will follow him as water pours into a broken ship.

Sutta-Nipata, iv, 1, 4.

15. Even if [after death] thou art attached to worldly goods left behind, thou will not be able to possess them, and they will be of no use to thee. Therefore, abandon weakness and attachment for them; cast them away wholly; renounce them from thy heart.

The Tibetan Book of the Dead, ii, 1.

16. What avail riches for the practice of religion?

Uttaradhyayana-Sutra, xiv, 17 (*Jainism*).

17. They make ropes of wet sand on the river bank, who rely on the riches of this earth.

Puran Singh, 87 (*Sikhism*).

18. Covet not the wealth of any man.

Isa Upanishad, 1.

19. Be thou free ... from the thought of getting and keeping.

KRISHNA. *Bhagavad-Gita*, ii, 45.

The Choice of Ways

26

The Free Choice of Ways

1. No man can serve two masters.

JESUS.   Matthew vi, 24.

2. I have set before thee life and death, the blessing and the curse: therefore choose life, that thou mayest live.

Deuteronomy xxx, 19 (R.V.).

3. Stand ye in the ways, and see, and ask for the old paths, where is the good way, and walk therein, and ye shall find rest for your souls.

Jeremiah vi, 16.

4. Before man is life and death; and whichsoever he liketh it shall be given him.

Ecclesiasticus xv, 17 (R.V.).

5. There are two Ways, one of Life and one of Death; but there is a great difference between the two Ways.

The Didache, i, 2.

6. Three grand operations of the mind of man: to think, to choose, and to perform.

Welsh Triad.

7. Three equiproportions to which man has the power of attaching himself as he pleases: Abred and Gwynvyd; necessity and liberty; evil and good.

Welsh Triad.

8. When God made man in his own likeness to be a perfectly free agent, he did it with so settled a purpose that he himself will not bring force to bear upon man.

KOMENSKY. *The Way of Light*, iv, 15.

9. In every one of us there are two ruling and directing principles . . . the one being an innate desire of pleasure; the other, an acquired judgment which aspires after excellence.

PLATO. *Phaedrus* (237).

10. The responsibility is on him that chooseth. There is none on God.

PLATO. *The Republic*, x, 15.

11. No man can at once love God and the carnal appetites.

PORPHYRY. *Letter to Marcella*, xiv.

12. Hear with your ears, and with your mind contemplate the flame, every man and woman ought to-day to choose his creed. Between the good and the base, in thought, word and deed choose one aright.

ZARATHUSHTRA. *The Avesta, Yasna*, xxx, 2, 3.

13. I pray thee to set before thyself the path that must be traversed.

The Wisdom of Ani, xv.

14. Decide beforehand what conduct should be, and then there will be no regrets: decide beforehand what the Way is, and then there will be no limit to the result.

TZU SSU. *The Doctrine of the Mean*, 20.

15. The ways are two: love and want of love. That is all.

Mencius, vii, 2.

16. The Way of Heaven and the Way of Man are far apart. They should be clearly distinguished from each other.

Kwang Tse, xi, 7.

17. Leave the path to the left and take the right-hand path. Go on for a little and you will see a thick forest. Go on for a little and you will see a great marshy swamp. Go on for a little and you will see a steep precipice. Go on for a little and you will see a delightful stretch of ground.

THE BUDDHA. *Samyutta-Nikaya,* iii, 106.

18. One is the road that leads to wealth, another the road that leads to Nirvana.

Dhammapada, 75.

19. There are two ways—one the love of God, the other of mammon.

Amar Das, ii, 167 *(Sikhism).*

20. The wise man chooses the better, indeed, rather than the pleasanter. The stupid man, from getting-and-keeping, chooses the pleasanter.

Katha Upanishad, ii, 2.

27

The Way lies Close at Hand

1. The kingdom of heaven is at hand.

JESUS.   *Matthew* iv, 17.

2. The Lord . . . be not far from every one of us.

PAUL.   *Acts* xvii, 27.

3. Behold, I stand at the door, and knock: if any man hear my voice, and open the door, I will come in to him.

Revelation iii, 20.

4. But the word is very nigh unto thee, in thy mouth, and in thy heart, that thou mayest do it.

MOSES.   *Deuteronomy* xxx, 14.

5. He shall find her [Wisdom] sitting at his doors.

Wisdom of Solomon vi, 14.

6. Oh, how happy men would be if they perceived that all those things which can make them happy are at their hand!

KOMENSKY.   *The Way of Light, Dedication*, 12.

7. Though the good is near, men neither see nor hear it.

Golden Verses of the Pythagoreans, 55.

8. Surely close at hand thou shalt light upon him; there are not so many things between thee and him.

PLOTINUS.   *Ennead*, v, 1, 3.

9. Without going out of his door, man can know the universe; without looking out of his window, man can perceive the heavenly Tao.

LAO TSE.   *Tao Teh King*, xlvii.

10. The Way is not far removed from men.

TZU SSU.   *The Doctrine of the Mean*, xiii, 1.

11. The way lies close at hand yet we seek for it afar.

Mencius, iv, 1, 11.

12. The Great Way of Tao . . . is not far from anyone.

HUAI NAN TSE.   *Yuen Tao Huin*, xviii.

28

The Kingdom of Heaven is Within Us

1. Neither shall they say, Lo here! or, lo, there! for behold, the kingdom of God is within you.

JESUS.   *Luke* xvii, 21.

2. The kingdom of Heaven is within you.

Extra-canonical Saying of Jesus (Oxyrhynchus papyrus, 654, 2).

3. Know ye not that ye are the temple of God, and that the Spirit of God dwelleth in you?

PAUL.   1 *Corinthians* iii, 16.

4. The Truth of things is within us and the Truth of the kingdom of God is for us.

KOMENSKY.   *The Way of Light, Dedication,* 31.

5. Thou has in thee something that is a portion of Him.

EPICTETUS.   *Dissertations,* ii, 8.

6. Cease to seek after God (as without thee), . . . seek Him from out of thyself, . . . thou wilt find Him in thyself, one and many, just as the atom; thus finding from thyself a way out of thyself.

MONOÏMUS.   *Letter to Theophrastus.*

7. God is not external to anyone, but is present with all things.

> PLOTINUS.   *Ennead*, vi, 9, 7.

8. Let thy temple be the mind that is within thee.

> PORPHYRY.   *Letter to Marcella*, xix.

9. I gazed into my own heart;
   There I saw Him; He was nowhere else.

> JALALU'D-DIN RUMI.   *Divani Shamsi Tabriz*.

10. He is the god Saä who is in your hearts.

> *The Teaching of Sehetepabra* (*Egyptian*).

11. These garments cover a jewel too precious for any barter of this world.

> LAO TSE, *reported by* VIN HI, *keeper of the Western Gate*.

12. Within yourselves deliverance must be sought.

> THE BUDDHA.   *The Light of Asia*, viii.

13. I am stationed within all beings. The wise know the father of all beings to be placed in the lotus-like heart of everyone.

> *Sanatsugativa*, vi.

14. Freedom from bonds is in your inmost heart.

> *Acharanga-Sutra*, i, 5, 2, 5 (*Jainism*).

15. God was concealed as a diamond in my heart.

> *Ram Das*, ii, 326 (*Sikhism*).

16. In the space within the heart are contained both heaven and earth.

Chandogya Upanishad, viii, 1, 3.

17. He who seeketh it shall find it—being grown perfect —in himself.

KRISHNA. *Bhagavad-Gita,* iv, 38.

Awakening and Revaluation

29

Ears that Hear

1. Go rather to the lost sheep of the house of Israel.

JESUS. *Matthew* x, 6.

2. The ear that heareth the reproof of life abideth among the wise.

Proverbs xv, 31.

3. Thine ears shall hear a word behind thee, saying, This is the way, walk ye in it, when ye turn to the right hand, and when ye turn to the left.

Isaiah xxx, 21.

4. I will seek that which was lost.

Ezekiel xxxiv, 16.

5. At the voice of it and at the sound of it, I started up from sleep, . . . and according to what was traced on my heart were the words of my letter written.

The Hymn of the Soul, 53 (*Acts of Thomas*, 108).

6. First, they made their force more formidable against Ear-gate; for they knew that unless they could penetrate that, no good could be done upon the town.

JOHN BUNYAN. *The Holy War*.

7. That man [Mr. Telltrue] so told the story of Christian and his travels, that my heart fell into a burning haste to be gone after him.

JOHN BUNYAN. *Pilgrim's Progress*, Part 2.

[95]

8. The truth which we possess . . . we will pass on to you at the least sign, and according to the measure of the capacity of each. Light is apt for communion, where there is reception and capacity, but it constrains no one, and waits its reception tranquilly.

ECKARTSHAUSEN.　*The Cloud upon the Sanctuary*, iii.

9. Our arguments are addressed to those who admit that there is another nature besides bodies, and who ascend [at least] as far as to soul.

PLOTINUS.　*Ennead*, vi, 9, 5.

10. Hear with your ears the best things.

ZARATHUSHTRA.　*The Avesta, Yasna*, v, 32.

11. This verily will convert many who are ready to hear.

ZARATHUSHTRA.　*The Avesta, Yasna*, xlvii, 6.

12. It is the heart of man that makes its possessor hear or not hear.

PTAH-HOTEP.　*Comments on his Teaching*, ii.

13. The teacher's way is no more than seeking our stray heart.

Mencius, xi, 11.

14. He who hath ears, let him hear the word and believe.

Vinaya, Mahavagga, i, 5, 12.

15. The knowledge of the things beneficial to the self is produced in one who sees and hears.

Anugita, xix.

16. It is called the Great Liberation by Hearing, because even those who have committed the five boundless sins are sure to be liberated if they hear it by the path of the ear.

The Tibetan Book of the Dead, i, 2.

17. It is with the mind that one hears.

Brihad-aranyaka Upanishad, i, 5, 3.

18. If many not possessing Memory should be assembled, indeed they would not hear any one at all, they would not think, they would not understand. But assuredly, if they should remember, then they would hear, then they would think, then they would understand.

Chandogya Upanishad, vii, 13, 1.

30

The Voice of
Memory and Conscience

1. One is your Master, even Christ.

JESUS.   *Matthew* xxiii, 10.

2. Moses . . . accounting the reproach of Christ greater riches than the treasures of Egypt.

Hebrews xi, 26 (R.*V.*).

3. The spirit of man is the candle of the Lord, searching all the inward parts.

Proverbs xx, 27.

4. It is the voice of my beloved that knocketh, saying, Open to me.

Song of Solomon v, 2.

5. The old gentleman [Mr. Conscience] . . . began to talk aloud, and his words were now to the town of Mansoul as if they were great claps of thunder.

JOHN BUNYAN.   *The Holy War.*

6. In it [the Metaphysical School] our objects, our Books and our Masters are not outside us, as in the Physical School, but within us. . . . To every man, learned and simple, wise and foolish, awake and asleep, these are constantly making their addresses, giving their teaching, their warning.

KOMENSKY.   *The Way of Light, Dedication*, 17.

7. The operation of the Holy Spirit does not take place at all in those things which are without life, or in those which, although living, are yet dumb; nay, is not found even in those who are endued indeed with reason, but are engaged in evil courses, and not at all converted to a better life. In those persons alone do I think that the operation of the Holy Spirit takes place, who are already turning to a better life.

ORIGEN. *De Principiis*, 1, iii, 5.

8. Good and evil, . . . what is our concern and what is not our concern, and what ought to be done and what not — who hath come into the world without an implanted notion of these things.

EPICTETUS. *Dissertations*, ii, 11.

9. With respect to memory, the body is an impediment to it; since even now oblivion is produced from the addition of certain things; but through oblation and purification, memory frequently emerges.

PLOTINUS. *Ennead*, iv, 3, 26.

10. I know Maät, which hath germinated, and hath become strong.

The Egyptian Book of the Dead, cxiv, 7.

11. You will not wait for the hearing of your ears about it, but for the hearing of your mind. You will not wait even for the hearing of your mind, but for the hearing of the breath of spirit.

Kwang Tse, iv, 2.

12. I am centred in the hearts of all, from me come memory and knowledge.

Krishna.   *Bhagavad-Gita*, xv, 15.

13.   Till at sunset Hiawatha,
Wounded, weary, and desponding, . . .
Paused to rest beneath a pine tree.
    Suddenly from the boughs above him
Sang the Mama, the woodpecker.

Hiawatha, ix.

3 1

Revaluation, Regeneration

1. Except a man be born again, he cannot see the kingdom of God.

JESUS.   John iii, 3.

2. As I made my journey, and was come nigh unto Damascus about noon, suddenly there shone from heaven a great light round about me. And I fell unto the ground, and heard a voice.

PAUL.   Acts xxii, 6.

3. All our righteousnesses are as filthy rags.

Isaiah lxiv, 6.

4. I saw a man clothed with rags, standing in a certain place, with his face from his own house.

JOHN BUNYAN.   Pilgrim's Progress, Part 1.

5. But the same day, as I was in the midst of a game at cat, and having struck it one blow from the hole, just as I was about to strike it a second time, a voice did suddenly dart from heaven into my soul.

JOHN BUNYAN.   Grace Abounding, 22.

6. I also found, the more I examined myself, that in my head there was only gross misunderstanding, and blindness in mysterious things . . . also that my bodily

behaviour, outward conversation, and brotherly love to-wards my neighbour was not duly purged and cleansed.

The Marriage of Christian Rosencreutz.

7. Rebirth is triple; there is, firstly, the rebirth of our intelligence; secondly, of our heart and our will; and finally, the rebirth of our entire being.

ECKARTSHAUSEN. *The Cloud upon the Sanctuary*, vi.

8. The beginning of philosophy, at least with those who lay hold of it as they ought and enter by the door, is the consciousness of their own feebleness and incapacity in respect of necessary things.

EPICTETUS. *Dissertations*, ii, 11, 1.

9. The true beauty of the world above is so brought to his remembrance that he begins to recover his plumage, and finding new wings, longs to soar aloft, but the power failing him, gazes upward like a bird, and becomes heedless of all lower matters.

PLATO. *Phaedrus* (249).

10. Whoso recognizes and confesses his own defects
    Is hastening in the way that leads to Perfection.

JALALU'D-DIN RUMI. *Masnavi.*

11. Homage to thee, O Governor of those who are in Amenti, who maketh mortals to be born again.

The Egyptian Book of the Dead, clxxxii, 16.

12. Count your rectitude as foolishness, know your cleverness to be stupidity.

LAO TSE. *Tao Teh King*, xlv.

13. ... becomes afterwards indifferent to all these, saying: "Enough of the births tending to actions, the fruits of which tend to bondage till the end of this mundane existence."

Mandalabrahmana Upanishad, ii.

14. What seems as wakeful day is known for night, thick night of ignorance, to his true-seeing eyes.

KRISHNA. *Bhagavad-Gita,* ii, 69.

15. "Master of Life," he cried, desponding,
    "Must our lives depend on these things?"

Hiawatha, v.

32

The Permanent and the Impermanent

1. The things which are seen are temporal; but the things which are not seen are eternal.

PAUL.   2 Corinthians iv, 18.

2. A man that could look no way but downwards, with a muck-rake in his hand. There stood also one over his head, with a celestial crown in his hand, and proffered him that crown for his muck-rake.

JOHN BUNYAN.   Pilgrim's Progress, Part 2.

3. There is a great difference between the external and the internal man; for the intellectuality of the former perishes, while the wisdom of the latter remains.

PARACELSUS.   De Fundamento Sapientiae.

4. All things of the senses are indeed trifles as compared with things of the mind, all bodily things as compared with things of the spirit, all temporal things as compared with eternal.

KOMENSKY.   The Way of Light, Dedication, 24.

5. There is a dual nature, one pure, spiritual, immortal and indestructible, the other impure, material, mortal and destructible.

ECKARTSHAUSEN.   The Cloud upon the Sanctuary, iv.

6. Those are philosophers who are able to grasp that which is always invariable and unchanging.

PLATO.   *The Republic*, vi, 1.

7. Whatsoever is material, doth soon vanish away into the common substance of the whole.

MARCUS AURELIUS.   *Meditations*, vii, 7.

8. In the beginning were established reality and non-reality.

ZARATHUSHTRA.   *The Avesta, Yasna*, xxx, 4.

9. The worldly existence is, in the end, death and disappearance, and of the spiritual existence, in the end, that of a soul of the righteous is undecaying, immortal, and undisturbed.

Menog-i Khrad, xl, 29–30 (*Zoroastrianism*).

10. If it is not of Tao, it will soon perish.

LAO TSE.   *Tao Teh King*, xxx.

11. The whole body of spiritual substance progresses without a pause; the whole body of material substance suffers decay without intermission.

LIEH TSE.

12. When you have understood the destruction of all that was made, you will understand that which was not made.

Dhammapada, 383.

13. Were there not this unborn, unoriginated, uncreated, unformed, there would be no escape from the world of the born, originated, created, formed.

THE BUDDHA.   *Udana*, viii, 1, 4, 3.

14. There are, assuredly, two forms of Brahma: the formed and the formless. Now, that which is the formed is unreal; that which is the formless is real, is Brahma, is light.

Maitri Upanishad, vi, 3.

15. In this world being is twofold: the Divided, one; the Undivided, one. All things that live are "the Divided." That which sits apart, "the Undivided."

KRISHNA.　*Bhagavad-Gita,* xv, 16.

33

True Wealth

1. Lay up for yourselves treasures in heaven, where neither moth nor rust doth corrupt, and where thieves do not break through nor steal.

Jesus. Matthew vi, 20.

2. There is that scattereth, and yet increaseth.

Proverbs xi, 24.

3. Thou hast much wealth if thou fear God.

Tobit iv, 21.

4. What is richer than Wisdom, that worketh all things?

Wisdom of Solomon viii, 5.

5. A man there was, though some did count him mad,
   The more he cast away, the more he had.

John Bunyan. Pilgrim's Progress, Part 2.

6. Grant that I may esteem wisdom the only riches, and may my store of gold be such as none but the good can bear.

Plato. Phaedrus (279).

7. To be self-sufficing is the greatest of all wealth.

Porphyry. Letter to Marcella, xxviii.

8. These are the people it is necessary to consider rich: the first is he who is perfect in wisdom.

Menog-i Khrad, xxxv, 3 (*Zoroastrianism*).

9. The wise man does not lay up treasure; his riches are within. . . . The more he gives to others, the more he has of his own.

LAO TSE.   *Tao Teh King*, lxxxi.

10. Who is able to take hold of his wealth in order to give it to men? Only he who has the Tao.

LAO TSE.   *Tao Teh King*, lxxvii.

11. One may pour into the "Heavenly Treasure-House" without its being filled; one may pour from it without its being exhausted.

Kwang Tse, ii, 7.

12. The treasure is that laid up . . . through charity and piety, temperance and self-control . . . the treasure thus hid is secure, and passes not away.

Nidhikanda-Sutta.

13. The riches of the liberal never waste away.

Rig Veda, x, 117, 1.

Self-Control

34

Ruling Oneself, before Ruling Others

1. Why beholdest thou the mote that is in thy brother's eye, but considerest not the beam that is in thine own eye?

JESUS.   *Matthew* vii, 3.

2. He that is slow to anger is better than the mighty; and he that ruleth his spirit than he that taketh a city.

Proverbs xvi, 32.

3. But if thou must yet rule and command, then rule thine own self. I give thee thy soul and body to rule as a kingdom.

KOMENSKY.   *The Labyrinth*, xxxix, 9.

4. The greatest thing is a strong rule, and of the greatest rulers he is best who first can rule himself.

APOLLONIUS OF TYANA.   *To Valerius.*

5. The heir to the kingdom ... [is taught] ... that he may become a king in reality by first governing his own appetites.

PLATO.   *The First Alcibiades.*

6. A very ridiculous thing it is, that a man should dispense with vice and wickedness in himself, which is in his power to restrain; and should go about to suppress it in others, which is altogether impossible.

MARCUS AURELIUS.   *Meditations*, vii, 41.

7. He who conquers others is strong, but he who conquers himself is mighty.

LAO TSE.   *Tao Teh King*, xxxiii.

8. The Master said "... when a man knows how to cultivate his self, it may be inferred that he knows how to rule other individuals."

TZU SSU.   *The Doctrine of the Mean*, 20.

9. There are many charges, but the charge of oneself is the root of all others.

Mencius, iv, 1, 19.

10. If one man conquer in battle a thousand times a thousand men, and if another conquer himself, he is the greatest of conquerors.

Dhammapada, 103.

11. Difficult to conquer is oneself. But when that is conquered everything is conquered.

Uttaradhyayana-Sutra, ix, 36 (*Jainism*).

12. Only he who has conquered his own senses can keep his subjects in obedience.

Laws of Manu, vii, 44.

35

Knowing Oneself

1. The kingdom of Heaven is within you; and whosoever shall know himself shall find it.

    Extra-canonical Saying of Jesus (Oxyrhynchus papyrus, 654, 2).

2. Examine yourselves, whether ye be in the faith; prove your own selves.

    PAUL.   2 *Corinthians* xiii, 5.

3. My son, prove thy soul in thy life, and see what is evil for it.

    Ecclesiasticus xxxvii, 27.

4. Three knowledges which appertain to wisdom: the knowledge of God, the knowledge of mankind, and the knowledge of one's own heart.

    Welsh Triad.

5. I have brought thee to thine own self.

    KOMENSKY.   *The Labyrinth,* xxxviii, 2.

6. Be persuaded by me and by the Delphic inscription, and "Know thyself" . . . and become acquainted with the soul.

    PLATO.   *The First Alcibiades.*

7. Diligently examine thyself concerning whatsoever thou doest.

    MARCUS AURELIUS.   *Meditations,* x, 37.

8. He who knows himself, will also know from whence he was derived.

Plotinus, vi, 9, 8.

9. He who knows others is discerning, but he who knows himself is enlightened.

Lao Tse. *Tao Teh King,* xxxiii.

10. He that goes to the bottom of his heart knows his own nature: and knowing his own nature he knows heaven.

Mencius, xiii, 1.

11. What I call happiness consists in the discovery of the true self.

Huai Nan Tse. *Yuen Tao Huin,* xix.

12. Examine thyself by thyself.

Dhammapada, 379.

13. The time hath now come for thee to seek the Path. ... At this moment, know thou thyself; and abide in that state.

The Tibetan Book of the Dead, i, 1.

14. Search in thy heart, search in thy heart of hearts.

Kabir, vi, 276 (*Sikhism*).

15. When we see, hear, perceive, and know the self, then all this is known.

Brihad-aranyaka Upanishad, ii, 5.

16. Speech is not what one should desire to understand. One should know the speaker. . . . The deed is not what one should desire to understand. One should know the doer. . . . Mind is not what one should desire to understand. One should know the thinker.

Kanshitaki Upanishad, iii, 8.

17. The ungoverned hath no knowledge of himself.

KRISHNA. *Bhagavad-Gita,* ii, 66.

36

Seeking the Real

1. But rather seek ye the kingdom of God.

JESUS. *Luke* xii, 31.

2. Gain for yourselves, by means of these transitory things which are not yours, that which is your own, and passeth not away.

Extra-canonical Saying of Jesus.

3. For we have not here an abiding city, but we seek after the city which is to come.

PAUL. *Hebrews* xiii, 14 (R.*V*.).

4. Set your affection on things above, not on things on the earth.

PAUL. *Colossians* iii, 2.

5. Depart from evil, and do good; seek peace and pursue it.

Psalm xxxiv, 14.

6. Cease to do evil; learn to do well.

Isaiah i, 16.

7. Seek out the wisdom of all the ancient.

Ecclesiasticus xxxix, 1.

8. We find that almost all men, fleeing outward from themselves, seek in the world and its things wherewith

[116]

to calm and quiet their minds. . . . I have learnt to seek
elsewhere the peace and security of my mind.

KOMENSKY. *The Labyrinth (Introduction)*.

9. If only man . . . would seek interiorly for a higher
principle, he would thereby approach that source which
alone can communicate this principle to all, because it is
wisdom in its essential substance.

ECKARTSHAUSEN. *The Cloud upon the Sanctuary*, i.

10. The true lover of learning naturally strove toward
what is, . . . until he grasped the nature of each reality
that is, with that part of his soul which is fitted to lay
hold of such by reason of its affinity with it.

PLATO. *The Republic*, vi, 5.

11. When the more exalted parts of us energize, and
the soul is elevated to natures better than itself, then it
is entirely separated from things which detain it in
generation.

IAMBLICHUS. *On the Mysteries*, viii, 7.

12. The righteous man wishes only to be there where
wisdom is at home.

ZARATHUSHTRA. *The Avesta, Yasna*, xxx, 9.

13. That one wish which Ahura Mazda, the Lord,
contemplates as regards men is this, that "ye shall fully
understand me; for every one who fully understands me,
comes after me and strives for my satisfaction."

Menog-i Khrad, xl, 24 (*Zoroastrianism*).

14. For things Divine are not accessible to mortals who fix their minds on body; 'tis they who strip them naked that speed aloft unto the Height.

Chaldean Oracles (Kroll 52).

15. Let not thyself abandon thy heart to the things that are extraneous.

The Teaching of Amen-em-apt, 165.

16. Hold fast the idea of "The Great."

LAO TSE. *Tao Teh King,* xxxv.

17. The truly wise rejoice in that which can never be lost, but endures always.

Kwang Tse, vi, 6.

18. Cease to do evil; learn to do good; cleanse thine own heart; this is the law of the Buddhas.

THE BUDDHA. *Dhammapada,* 183.

19. From the unreal lead me to the real! From darkness lead me to light!

Brihad-aranyaka Upanishad, i, 3, 28.

20. With means which are inconstant I have obtained that which is constant.

Katha Upanishad, ii, 10.

37

Cleansing

1. Cleanse first that which is within.

> JESUS.   *Matthew* xxiii, 26.

2. Let us cleanse ourselves from all filthiness of the flesh and spirit.

> PAUL.   *2 Corinthians* vii, 1.

3. Wash me and I shall be whiter than snow.

> *Psalm* li, 7.

4. Wash you, make you clean; put away the evil of your doings from before mine eyes.

> *Isaiah* i, 16.

5. I will put these stones, being cleansed, into the tower.

> *The Shepherd of Hermas, Similitudes,* ix, 61.

6. Have them into the garden to the bath, and there wash them, and make them clean from the soil which they have gathered by travelling.

> JOHN BUNYAN.   *Pilgrim's Progress,* Part 2.

7. True virtue is a complete purification from all the leading passions; and temperance, justice, fortitude, and wisdom itself form this purification.

> PLATO.   *Phaedo* (69).

8. All the virtues are purifications, and necessarily consist in the soul being purified ... this is the life which is the principal and leading aim of a worthy man.

PLOTINUS.   *Ennead*, ii, 2, 7.

9. Purity, for him who cleanses his own self with good actions, words and deeds.

The Avesta, Vendidad, v, 21.

10. Soil not the spirit, and deepen not the plane.

Chaldean Oracles (Kroll 64).

11. Verily I have cleansed my soul. ... I have made myself clean in the Lake of Making to be at Peace, and in the Lake of Weighing in the Balance.

The Egyptian Book of the Dead, xcvii, 7.

12. Destroying sin by merit, he has his self illuminated by knowledge.

Sanatsugativa, iii, 8.

13. The law is my pond, ... having bathed in this pond I shall become clean, pure, thoroughly cooled, and shall at once relinquish all hatred.

Nirgrantha-Pravachana, iv, 24 (*Jainism*).

14. The body is cleansed by water, the mind by truthfulness, the individual soul by sacred learning and austerities, the intellect by true knowledge.

Laws of Manu, v, 109.

15. The flame of Knowledge wastes works' dross away. There is no purifier like thereto in all this world.

KRISHNA.   *Bhagavad-Gita*, iv, 37–38.

38

Following Intuition and Obeying Conscience

1. Grieve not the Holy Spirit which is in you, and put not out the Light which hath shone forth in you.

Extra-canonical Saying of Jesus.

2. By the obedience of one, shall many be made righteous.

PAUL. *Romans* v, 19.

3. The fear of the Lord is the beginning of wisdom.

Proverbs ix, 10.

4. Walk in the ways of thine heart.

Ecclesiastes xi, 9.

5. Walk in the light of your own fire, and in the flame which ye have kindled.

Isaiah l, 11 (*Origen*).

6. Let the counsel of thine own heart stand: for there is no man more faithful unto thee than it.

Ecclesiasticus xxxvii, 13.

7. As for Mr. Recorder [whose name was Mr. Conscience], before the town was taken he was a man well read in the laws of his King.

JOHN BUNYAN. *The Holy War.*

8. Those who are truly subject to God heed but their own conscience; what it forbids them they do not, but they do that which it tells them they may do.

KOMENSKY. *The Labyrinth*, xliv, 3.

9. It is plain and easy, if by the help of the Magnet, thou turnest neither to the left nor right.

The Marriage of Christian Rosencreutz.

10. But most of all respect thyself.

Golden Verses of the Pythagoreans, 12.

11. Knowledge is a noble and commanding thing, which cannot be overcome, and will not allow a man, if he only knows the difference of good and evil, to do anything contrary to knowledge.

PLATO. *Protagoras* (352).

12. By the glow of Fire the vigour of good thought has come to me.

ZARATHUSHTRA. *The Avesta, Yasna*, xliii, 4.

13. He who hears the inner voice within him has no need to listen to outside words.

JALALU'D-DIN RUMI. *Masnavi.*

14. Guide thou to me my heart at the season when there is cloud and darkness.

The Egyptian Book of the Dead, xxi.

15. Follow thine heart so long as thou livest, and do no more than is said.

The Teaching of Ptah-hotep, xi.

16. I am a man who hearkens; I hearken to Maät and, indeed, cause it to declare its message to my heart.

The Philosophy of Antef, 13 (*British Museum stele,* 197).

17. The heart of the self-controlled man is always in the Inner Kingdom.

LAO TSE.   *Tao Teh King,* xlix.

18. The feeling of right and wrong is the origin of wisdom.

Mencius, iii, 6.

19. The standard of conduct lies with one's own self; the testing of it lies with other men. . . . He who does not follow Tao when standard and test are both clear may be likened to one who, when leaving a house, does not go by the door, or, when travelling abroad, does not keep to the straight road.

LIEH TSE.

20. Those alone who are guided by their intuitions find the true standard.

Kwang Tse, xvii, 7.

21. Be ye lamps unto yourselves.

Digha-Nikaya, Maha-Parinibbana Sutta, ii, 33.

22. Accept not because it is in the scriptures, by mere logic, nor by inference, nor by consideration of appearances. . . . But, if at any time you know of yourself—"these are sinful conditions, these are wrongful . . ." then eschew them.

Anguttara-Nikaya, Tetrads, 192.

23. There is one instructor; there is no second different from him. I speak concerning him who abides in the heart.

Anugita, xi.

24. This above all,—To thine own self be true;
    And it shall follow as the night the day,
    Thou canst not then be false to any man.

SHAKESPEARE.   *Hamlet,* i, 3.

39

Control of Thought and Emotion

1. Bringing into captivity every thought to the obedience of Christ.

PAUL.   2 Corinthians x, 5.

2. Let not the sun go down upon your wrath.

PAUL.   Ephesians iv, 26.

3. Thou shalt not make unto thee any graven image, or the likeness of any thing.

Exodus xx, 4 (R.V.).

4. Surely I have stilled and quieted my soul; like a weaned child.

Psalm cxxxi, 2 (R.V.).

5. There are three things with which wisdom cannot exist: covetousness, licentiousness, and pride.

Welsh Triad.

6. For here lay the excellent wisdom of him that built Mansoul, that the walls could never be broken down nor hurt by the most mighty adverse potentate, unless the townsmen gave consent thereto.

JOHN BUNYAN.   The Holy War.

7. Religion tends always towards the subjection of the senses, . . . because it desires to make the spiritual man

dominant, in order that the truly rational man may govern the man of sense.

ECKARTSHAUSEN. *The Cloud upon the Sanctuary*, i.

8. The Essenes reject pleasures as an evil, but esteem continence, and the conquest over our passions, to be virtue. . . . They dispense their anger after a just manner, and restrain their passion.

JOSEPHUS. *Wars of the Jews*, ii, 8, 2–6.

9. Our duty is to show ourselves rulers over the inferior creation within us, gaining the mastery by means of our rational principle.

ISIDORUS. *On an Appended Soul.*

10. The rational part [of the soul] should rule . . . and the spirited part should be its subject and ally. . . . And these two so nurtured, truly taught and trained in their own offices, will be set over the desiring element.

PLATO. *The Republic*, iv, 17.

11. Whosoever they be that intend not and guide not by reason and discretion the motions of their own souls, they must of necessity be unhappy.

MARCUS AURELIUS. *Meditations*, ii, 5.

12. Every passion of the soul makes against our salvation.

PORPHYRY. *Letter to Marcella*, ix.

13. Desires are to be discriminated by us who are men and women, for our own selves.

Pahlavi Yasna, xxx, 2.

14. He has gained nothing who has not gained the soul.

Fragments (Darmesteter), 3 (Zoroastrianism).

15. The mortal once endowed with Mind must on his soul put bridle, in order that it may not plunge into the ill-starred Earth but win to freedom.

Chaldean Oracles (Kroll 52).

16. Empty thyself from that which is caused by thy desire; then advance towards thy Master.

BAHA-U-LLAH. *The Seven Valleys.*

17. Be weighty in thy mind, consolidate thy heart, accustom not thyself to shape thy course by thy tongue.

The Teaching of Amen-em-apt (385–386).

18. The self-controlled man governs by stilling the emotions, by quieting thought, by mastering the will, by increasing strength.

LAO TSE. *Tao Teh King, iii.*

19. No food is better for the heart than few desires.

Mencius, vii, 2, 35.

20. The spirit of man loves purity, but his mind disturbs it. The mind of man loves stillness, but his desires draw it away. If he could always send his desires away, his mind would of itself become still. Let his mind be made clean, and his spirit will of itself become pure.

Khing Kang King (The Classic of Purity), 3.

21. Such things as enter from without will never cease to flow in as long as there is no resolution to control the receptivity—the wishes, intentions and desires.

HUAI NAN TSE. *Yuen Tao Huin*, xx.

22. Good it is to tame the mind, so difficult to control, fickle and capricious.

Dhammapada, 35.

23. He who holds back rising anger like a rolling chariot, him I call a real driver; other people are but holding the reins.

Dhammapada, 222.

24. He whose mind is not shaken by contact with the things of the world . . . that is a supreme blessing.

Sutta-Nipata, ii, 4, 11.

25. This world is a bridge; pass over it, but build no house there.

Carving over the Gate of the Mosque at Fatehpur Sikri.

26. Again and again it should be reflected . . . that too much attachment to things should be avoided.

Tattvartha-Sutra, ix, 7 (*Jainism*).

27. He whose speech and mind are pure and ever properly guarded, obtains the whole reward recognized by the canons of the Veda.

Laws of Manu, ii, 160.

28. He who has understanding, whose mind is constantly held firm—his senses are under control, like the good horses of a chariot driver.

Katha Upanishad, iii, 6.

29. That man is wise who keeps the mastery of his senses.

KRISHNA.   *Bhagavad-Gita*, ii, 61.

40

Being Unaffected by Externals

1. See that ye be not troubled.

JESUS.   *Matthew* xxiv, 6.

2. Unto the pure all things are pure.

PAUL.   *Titus* i, 15.

3. Man has the power of self-control, and no external influences can control him if he exercises this power.

PARACELSUS.   *De Natura Rerum.*

4. And be that tower of strength that will not shake Altho' its top is harassed by the wind.

DANTE.   *Purgatorio*, v, 4.

5. Would not the bravest and wisest soul be least disturbed or altered by any outside effect?

PLATO.   *The Republic*, ii, 20.

6. To a good man nothing is evil.

PLATO.   *Apology of Socrates*, xxxiii.

7. If therefore it be a thing external that causes thy grief, know, that it is not that properly that doth cause it, but thine own conceit and opinion concerning the things which thou mayest rid thyself of, when thou wilt.

MARCUS AURELIUS.   *Meditations*, viii, 45.

8. May Anubis make my thighs firm so that I may stand thereon.

The Egyptian Book of the Dead, xxvi, 6.

9. The wise man is concerned with inner things, he is not concerned with outer things.

LAO TSE. *Tao Teh King,* xii.

10. The nobler type of man, while constantly solicitous, never suffers grief of any duration. . . . Even if some transient cause for grief were to come his way, he would not regard it as such.

Mencius.

11. Let externals take care of themselves. . . . Be still, as though pure.

Kwang Tse, xxxiii.

12. The Sage does not permit his body to be under the control of external influences, nor does he permit lusts to throw into confusion the harmony which reigns within him.

HUAI NAN TSE. *Yuen Tao Huin,* xix.

13. By restraint and control, the wise man may make for himself an island which no flood can overwhelm.

Dhammapada, 25.

14. For that which clingeth to another thing there is a fall: but unto that which clingeth not no fall can come. Where no fall cometh, there is rest.

THE BUDDHA. *Udana,* viii, 1, 4, 3.

15. He whose soul is not attached to external objects obtaineth the happiness that is in one's self.

KRISHNA.　*Bhagavad-Gita*, v, 21.

41

Moderation and Balance

1. Every man that striveth for the mastery is temperate in all things.

PAUL. 1 Corinthians ix, 25.

2. Let your moderation be known unto all men.

PAUL. Philippians iv, 5.

3. Measure in all things is best.

Golden Verses of the Pythagoreans, 38.

4. Temperance ... which consists in not being transported by the passions, but in controlling them with coolness and moderation.

PLATO. Phaedo (68).

5. Excessive pleasures and pains are what we should deem the greatest diseases of the soul:—for when a man is over-elevated with joy or unduly depressed with grief, and so hastens immoderately either to retain the one or fly from the other, he can neither perceive nor hear anything properly, but is agitated with fury, and very little capable of exercising the reasoning power.

PLATO. Timaeus, lxviii.

6. Whether thou hearest the thing that is good or the thing that is evil, treat it as a matter that is outside thy interest; hearken not to it.

The Teaching of Amen-em-apt, 202, 3.

7. Moderation is desirable in every affair.

BAHA-U-LLAH.   *Words of Paradise.*

8. [The wise man] is not affected by favour or disgrace, he is beyond consideration of profit or loss, he regards alike honour and contempt.

LAO TSE.   *Tao Teh King,* lvi.

9. I know why the Way is not pursued: the learned run to excess and the ignorant fall short, . . . the good run to excess and the bad fall short.

TZU SSU.   *The Doctrine of the Mean,* 4.

10. Honour and dishonour, success and failure, openness and scheming, frankness and deceit: with these pairs of opposites how can we avoid troubles? The middle way of achievement is found only in Tao.

Kwang Tse, xx, 1.

11. The height of virtue is an absence of both joy and sorrow from the heart; the height of tranquillity is to reach this condition and abide in it without change.

HUAI NAN TSE.   *Yuen Tao Huin,* xvii.

12. Devotion to the pleasures of sense—devotion to self-mortification: by avoiding these two extremes he who hath won the Truth has gained knowledge of that Middle Path which giveth vision.

THE BUDDHA.   *Samyutta-Nikaya,* v, 421.

13. Let a man cultivate equanimity.

Sutta-Nipata, iii, 11, 24.

14. To be free from repulsion and attraction, or from the wish to take or to avoid,—to enter in the mood of complete impartiality,—is the most profound of arts.

The Tibetan Book of the Dead, ii, 2.

15. Seeing prosperity, one should not be joyful; seeing misfortune, one should not weep. As prosperity is, so is misfortune; what is arranged by destiny, that happens.

Kabir, 478 (*Sikhism*).

16. Who, unto friend and foe keeping an equal heart, with equal mind bears shame and glory; with an equal peace takes heat and cold, pleasure and pain, . . . that man I love.

KRISHNA. *Bhagavad-Gita*, xii, 13.

Action

42

Doing, as well as Hearing and Speaking

1. If ye know these things, blessed are ye if ye do them.

JESUS.   *John* xiii, 17 (R.*V*.).

2. Everyone that heareth these sayings of mine, and doeth them not, shall be likened unto a foolish man, which built his house upon the sand.

JESUS.   *Matthew* vii, 26.

3. The kingdom of God is not in word, but in power.

PAUL.   1 *Corinthians* iv, 20.

4. Be doers of the word not hearers only.

James i, 22.

5. It were better for them not to have known the way of righteousness, than, after knowing it, to turn back.

2 *Peter* ii, 21 (R.*V*.).

6. Three things must be united before good can come of them: thinking well, speaking well, acting well.

Welsh Triad.

7. Hearing is but as the sowing of the seed; talking is not sufficient to prove that fruit is indeed in the heart and life.

JOHN BUNYAN.   *Pilgrim's Progress*, Part 1.

8. When I hear a man discoursing of wisdom ... I compare the man and his words, and note the harmony and correspondence of them.

PLATO.   *Laches* (188).

9. Whosoever holds a belief must live in accordance with it. God prizes not the words of the wise man, but his deeds.

PORPHYRY.   *Letter to Marcella*, viii and xvi.

10. Of heaven the first part is that of good thoughts, the second is that of good words, and the third is that of good deeds.

Menog-i Khrad, vii, 12 (*Zoroastrianism*).

11. When souls of great experience hear of Tao, diligently they put it into practice.

LAO TSE.   *Tao Teh King*, xli.

12. It is not the knowing that is difficult, but the doing.

Shu King, iv, 8.

13. Let a man make himself what he preaches to others.

Dhammapada, 159.

14. Clever talking will not work salvation.

Uttaradhyayana-Sutra, vi, 10 (*Jainism*).

15. How shalt thou be saved without good works?

Nanak, i, 351 (*Sikhism*).

16. Let a wise Brahman, after he has discovered him [the Self], practise wisdom.

Brihad-aranyaka Upanishad, iv, 4, 21.

17. Ponder it well in thy mind, and then act as it seemeth best unto thee.

KRISHNA.   *Bhagavad-Gita*, xviii, 63.

43

Doing One's Allotted Task

1. Render therefore unto Caesar the things that are Caesar's; and unto God the things that are God's.

JESUS. *Matthew* xxii, 21.

2. Submit yourselves to every ordinance of man for the Lord's sake.

1 *Peter* ii, 13.

3. Whatsoever thy hand findeth to do, do it with thy might.

Ecclesiastes ix, 10.

4. Whatsoever is brought unto thee take cheerfully.

Ecclesiasticus ii, 4.

5. As to thy burden, be content to bear it, until thou comest to the place of deliverance; for there it will fall from thy back of itself.

JOHN BUNYAN. *Pilgrim's Progress,* Part 1.

6. Serve with thy soul me alone, with thy body him whom thou canst or must.

KOMENSKY. *The Labyrinth,* liii.

7. Be satisfied with your business, and learn to love what you were bred to; and as to the remainder of your life, be entirely resigned, and let the gods do their pleasure.

MARCUS AURELIUS. *Meditations,* x, 12.

8. To resist him that is set in authority is evil.

The Teaching of Ptah-hotep, xxxi.

9. He who has Teh attends to his own obligations under the contract; he who has not Teh attends only to his rights under the contract.

LAO TSE. *Tao Teh King*, lxxix.

10. The acts of the true man agree with the station in life in which he finds himself, and he is not concerned with matters outside that station.

TZU SSU. *The Doctrine of the Mean*, 14.

11. Nothing comes unbidden. We must obey and accept our own true bidding.

Mencius, xiii, 2.

12. Let no one forget his own duty for the sake of another's, however great.

Dhammapada, 166.

13. Let him avoid all undertakings (the success of which) depends on others; but let him eagerly pursue that (the accomplishment of) which depends on himself.

Laws of Manu, iv, 159.

14. Giving up passions . . . he does only those he is asked to do.

Mandalabrahmana Upanishad, ii.

15. Perform thine allotted task with detachment, since in performance of his task without attachment man will attain to the highest.

KRISHNA. *Bhagavad-Gita*, iii, 19.

44

Accounting for Our Actions

1. Every idle word that men shall speak, they shall give account thereof in the day of judgment.

JESUS.   Matthew xii, 36.

2. Each man's work shall be made manifest; for the day shall declare it, because it is revealed in fire; and the fire itself shall prove each man's work of what sort it is.

PAUL.   1 Corinthians iii, 13 (R.V.).

3. Rejoice, O young man, in thy youth . . . but know that for all these things God will bring thee unto judgment.

Ecclesiastes xi, 9.

4. Man is a being capable of choice, and judgment will be given upon him and his acts. . . . it is right that he should receive punishment or reward as his works require.

Barddas (Welsh MS.).

5. Scales shall be fixed . . . whereby each one shall lightly find what he hath left at home behind.

The Marriage of Christian Rosencreutz.

6. Their own soul and their own self shall torment them when they come to the Bridge of the Separator.

ZARATHUSHTRA.   The Avesta, Yasna, xlvi, 11.

7. Be kind to thyself, make thy body strong and happy, but take good heed to thyself in respect of Nebertcher.

The Teaching of Amen-em-apt, 147.

8. Remember the Assessors who judge wrongdoers. Know that they will not be lenient on that day of judgment.

The Teaching of King Khati, xiii.

9. If they offend against Heaven, there is no place where they can take refuge.

Mo Tse, xxviii.

10. The Good Genius, who was born simultaneously with thee, will now come and count out thy good deeds with white pebbles, and the Evil Genius, who was born simultaneously with thee, will come and count out thy evil deeds with black pebbles. . . . Then the Lord of Death will say "I will consult the Mirror of Karma, . . . wherein every good and evil act is vividly reflected."

The Tibetan Book of the Dead, ii, 1 (*The Judgment*).

11. In the next world they place his good and evil deeds in a balance. . . . Now whosoever knows this places himself in the balance in this world.

Satapatha Brahmana, xi, 2, 7, 33.

45

Acting without Thought of the Reward

1. Take heed that ye do not your righteousness before men, to be seen of them.

JESUS.   Matthew vi, 1 (R.V.).

2. Then said the Interpreter again, "Fruit, you see, is that thing you look for, ... beware that in this you condemn not yourselves."

JOHN BUNYAN.   Pilgrim's Progress, Part 2.

3. Thou therefore must be one of them, who what they do, barely do it without any further thought.

MARCUS AURELIUS.   Meditations, v, 6.

4. Teach us, Asha, ... the law of the profitable, in which he who does right from purity, finds it well with him.

The Avesta, Yasna, xxxiv, 13.

5. The wise man acts without expectation of reward and completes his task without claiming merit.

LAO TSE.   Tao Teh King, lxxvii.

6. The nobler type of man simply acts according to the rule of right, and then awaits whatever may be ordained.

Mencius, xiv, 33.

7. There should not be the practice of what is good with any thought of the fame which it will bring.

Kwang Tse, iii, 1.

8. To bestow favours without seeking for a return, and give to others without any subsequent regret: this is what is called a good man.

Kan Ying Phien, 3.

9. This holy life is not practised ... for the purpose of gain, benefit or fame.

Anguttara-Nikaya, Tetrads, 26.

10. If I still go on feeling attraction and repulsion, then shall I wander in endless Sangsara [birth and death]. ... Henceforth I will never act through attraction and re-pulsion.

The Tibetan Book of the Dead, ii, 2.

11. To act solely from a desire for rewards is not laudable.

Laws of Manu, ii, 2.

12. Let right deeds be thy motive, not the fruit which comes from them.

KRISHNA. *Bhagavad-Gita*, ii, 47.

46

Singleness of Purpose; Freedom from Anxiety

1. Consider the lilies of the field, how they grow; they toil not, neither do they spin.

JESUS.   Matthew vi, 28.

2. In nothing be anxious.

PAUL.   Philippians iv, 6 (R.V.).

3. In singleness of heart seek ye him.

Wisdom of Solomon i, 1.

4. Keep that light in your eye, and go up directly thereto: so shalt thou see the gate.

JOHN BUNYAN.   Pilgrim's Progress, Part 1.

5. And as a child will stretch its arms in fond desire
   Towards the parent whence it nurture drew,
   So does the soul, that flame has touched, aspire.

DANTE.   Paradiso, xxiii, 25.

6. Weary not thyself concerning the affairs of the day, nor be anxious overmuch about thy house and estate.

The Teaching of Ptah-hotep, xi.

7. He who has his foundation in Teh is like a little child.

LAO TSE.   Tao Teh King, lv.

8. The great man is one who has never lost the heart of a child.

Mencius, iv, 2, 12.

9. It is only the path of pure simplicity which guards and preserves the Spirit.

Kwang Tse, xv, 3.

10. Good people walk on whatever befall.

Dhammapada, 83.

11. Be not distracted. . . . If thou givest way to indecision for even a second, thou wilt have to suffer misery for a long, long time. . . . Hold fast to one single purpose. Persistently join up the chain of good acts.

The Tibetan Book of the Dead, ii, 2.

12. Let a Brahman become disgusted with learning and desire to live as a child.

Brihad-aranyaka Upanishad, iii, 5.

13. Fearlessness, singleness of soul, the will always to strive for wisdom . . . be the signs of him whose feet are set on that fair path which leads to heavenly birth.

KRISHNA. *Bhagavad-Gita*, xvi, 1–3.

47

It is the Motive that Counts

1. For, as he thinketh in his heart, so is he.

Proverbs xxiii, 7.

2. The thought of foolishness is sin.

Proverbs xxiv, 9.

3. Whosoever looketh on a woman to lust after her hath committed adultery with her already in his heart.

JESUS. *Matthew* v, 28.

4. No action, as such, is either good or bad, ... but its character depends on how it is performed.

PLATO. *The Symposium* (181).

5. Things are indifferent, but the uses of them are not indifferent.

EPICTETUS. *Dissertations*, ii, 5, i.

6. Woe to the giver who gives for the joy of his ·own soul.

Nirangistan Nask, 84 (*Zoroastrianism*).

7. For whatever purpose a man bestows any gift, for that same purpose he receives in his next birth, with due honour, its reward.

Laws of Manu, iv, 234.

8. The right act is less, far less, than the right-thinking mind.

KRISHNA.   *Bhagavad-Gita,* ii, 49.

48

The Necessity for Effort and Care

1. Seek, and ye shall find; knock, and it shall be opened unto you.

Jesus.   Matthew vii, 7.

2. Ye shall seek me and find me, when ye shall search for me with all your heart.

Jeremiah xxix, 13.

3. Those that seek me diligently shall find me.

Proverbs viii, 17 (R.V.).

4. Search, and seek, and she [Wisdom] shall be made known unto thee; and when thou hast got hold of her, let her not go.

Ecclesiasticus vi, 27.

5. The three efforts of wisdom: to understand nature by the light which is divine, to see the truth by searching into it, and to exercise love and peace.

Welsh Triad.

6. Do you not remember that one of the Shepherds bid us beware of the Enchanted Ground? He meant by that, that we should beware of sleeping.

John Bunyan.   Pilgrim's Progress, Part 1.

7. He who said "Seek," also said "Knock and seek." It is not, then, the will of God that . . . we should ask or wait

without making an effort of our own.

> KOMENSKY. *The Way of Light*, vii, 3.

8. Her servants let down a cord seven times into the dungeon and drew up whomsoever could hang thereon.

> *The Marriage of Christian Rosencreutz.*

9. "Hardly can a man become good, for the gods have made virtue the reward of toil."

> PLATO (*quoting* HESIOD). *Protagoras* (340).

10. He that would return to the gods from the foreign land in which we dwell must abandon pleasure and levity, and must strenuously climb as if ascending a high mountain.

> PORPHYRY. *Letter to Marcella*, vi.

11. Every good work which thou art able to do to-day do not postpone for to-morrow, and accomplish with thine own hand the counsel of thine own soul.

> *Sar Dar*, lxxxi, 10 (*Zoroastrianism*).

12. In order to succeed, strive and exert yourselves. If you strive not for your objects, ye are fools.

> JALALU'D-DIN RUMI. *Masnavi.*

13. Be active, with the Activity of Inner Life.

> LAO TSE. *Tao Teh King*, lxiii.

14. The path may not be left for an instant. If it could be left, it would not be the path. On this account, the superior man does not wait till he sees things, to be cautious, nor till he hears things, to be apprehensive.

> TZU SSU. *The Doctrine of the Mean*, i, 2.

15. The way is like the high road, nowise hard to know. Man's sickness is in not seeking it. Go home, Sir, and seek it. There are teachers and to spare.

Mencius, xii, 2.

16. Three things hinder Tao: to see the good to be done and to neglect it; to hesitate when the occasion presents itself; and to know evil and follow it.

Tze Ya Tze.

17. Do ye abide in heedfulness.

The Buddha. *Digha-Nikaya,* ii, 154.

18. Ye must exert yourselves, holding to the thought of "This is ill; this is the cause of ill; this is the ceasing of ill; this is the way leading to the ceasing of ill." Thus, brethren, must ye exert yourselves.

The Buddha. *Samyutta-Nikaya,* v, 455.

19. If anything is to be done, let a man do it, let him attack it vigorously.

Dhammapada, 313.

20. It hath been said, "Exert thine energy to the utmost": this is needed now.

The Tibetan Book of the Dead, ii, 2.

21. Exert and control yourself.

Sutra-Kritanga, i, 2, 1, 11 (*Jainism*).

22. Steadfastly the will must toil to wisdom.

Krishna. *Bhagavad-Gita,* vi, 23.

49

Dependence upon One's Own Efforts

----

1. Whosoever doth not bear his own cross, and come after me, cannot be my disciple.

JESUS.   *Luke* xiv, 27 (R.*V*.).

2. For every man shall bear his own burden.

PAUL.   *Galatians* vi, 5.

3. Work out your own salvation.

PAUL.   *Philippians* ii, 12.

4. And Jacob was left alone, and there wrestled a man with him until the breaking of the day.

Genesis xxxii, 24.

5. Moses said, "This people have sinned a great sin . . . blot me, I pray thee, out of thy book which thou hast written." And the Lord said unto Moses, "Whosoever hath sinned against me, him will I blot out of my book."

Exodus xxxii, 31–33.

6. They put together a load both great and light, that I might carry it alone.

The Hymn of the Soul, 4 (*Acts of Thomas,* 108).

7. For a Christian can never be overcome, unless he should yield of himself.

JOHN BUNYAN.   *Pilgrim's Progress,* Part 2.

8. Being has this necessary peculiarity, that its change is brought about by nothing external to itself.

APOLLONIUS OF TYANA.   *To Valerius.*

9. The Saviour saith "Save thyself, thou and thy soul."

CLEMENT OF ALEXANDRIA.   *Excerpts from Theodotus,* ii.

10. Virtue therefore must be a thing which cannot be taught.

PLATO.   *Meno* (96).

11. Every man's happiness depends from himself.

MARCUS AURELIUS.   *Meditations,* ii, 3.

12. The skill which souls derive from experience is sufficient to their salvation.

Plotinus, ii, 9, 5.

13. With one's own strength one becomes independent.

ZARATHUSHTRA.   *The Avesta, Yasna,* ix, 25.

14. In the end thy trust is on thine own deeds.

Menog-i Khrad, ii, 108 (*Zoroastrianism*).

15. I have opened up a way for myself.

The Egyptian Book of the Dead, lxxii.

16. All beings will be transformed from within themselves.

LAO TSE.   *Tao Teh King,* xxxvii.

17. As the Master said "In archery . . . if a man misses the target, he looks for the cause in himself."

TZU SSU.   *The Doctrine of the Mean,* 14.

18. Whenever our actions fail to produce the effect desired, we should look for the cause in ourselves.

Mencius, vii, 4.

19. If Tao could be communicated, who would not endeavour to present it to his ruler, to his parents, and to those dear to him.

Kwang Tse, xiv, 5.

20. Work out your salvation with diligence.

THE BUDDHA. *Mahaparinivana-Sutta*, vi, 10.

21. You yourself must make an effort. The Buddhas can only show the way.

Dhammapada, 276.

22. The way to which ... is to be crossed by one singly.

Anugita, xii.

23. Alone he accumulates merit; alone he enjoys the happiness of heaven; alone he destroys karma; alone also he attains to liberation.

Twelve Meditations, 14 (*Jainism*).

24. Depend not on another, rather lean upon thyself, trust to thine own exertions.

Laws of Manu, iv, 160.

25. Let each man raise himself by self.

KRISHNA. *Bhagavad-Gita*, vi, 5.

True Teachers

50

The Master is generally Unrecognized

---

1. No prophet is accepted in his own country.

JESUS.   *Luke* iv, 24.

2. He came unto his own, and his own received him not.

John i, 11.

3. For it is a thing very possible, that a man should be a very divine man, and yet be altogether unknown.

MARCUS AURELIUS.   *Meditations*, vii, 38.

4. I am forsaken by kinsmen and nobles; neither do my people like me.

ZARATHUSHTRA.   *The Avesta, Yasna*, xlvi, 1.

5. Few there are who know me.

LAO TSE.   *Tao Teh King*, lxx.

6. This deluded world knows me not.

KRISHNA.   *Bhagavad-Gita*, vii, 25.

51

Veritable Teachers

1. He taught them as one having authority.

Matthew vii, 29.

2. To this end am I come into the world, that I should bear witness unto the truth.

JESUS.   *John* xviii, 37 (R.*V*.).

3. Let a man so account of us, as of ministers of Christ, and stewards of the mysteries of God.

PAUL.   1 *Corinthians* iv, 1 (R.*V*.).

4. I stood between the Lord and you at that time, to show you the word of the Lord.

MOSES.   *Deuteronomy* v, 5.

5. The Lord hath given me the tongue of them that are taught, that I should know how to speak a word in season to him that is weary.

Isaiah 1, 4 (R.*V*.).

6. In all time there have been men illuminated of God who had this interior knowledge of the things of faith demonstrated objectively.

ECKARTSHAUSEN.   *The Cloud upon the Sanctuary*, iv.

7. The Theurapeutae preserve an unbroken memory of God.... Hence many of them give out the rhythmic doctrines of the sacred wisdom, which they have obtained in the visions of dream-life.

PHILO. *On the Contemplative Life.*

8. Before that time [when Jesus Christ became man and was tabernacled in the flesh], Christ, the Word of God, was in Moses and the prophets.

ORIGEN. *De Principiis (Preface).*

9. We must trust to the reports of those ancient men ... and as they declare that they are relating matters with which they are familiarly acquainted, we ought to assent to their tradition.

PLATO. *Timaeus,* xvi.

10. The word of the Master ... overpasses speech and writing.

PLOTINUS. *Ennead,* vi, 9, 4.

11. May the Creator of Wisdom teach me his ordinances through good thought, that my tongue may have a pathway.

ZARATHUSHTRA. *The Avesta, Yasna,* 1, 6.

12. I have opened fair things in my name of "Opener of the road."

The Egyptian Book of the Dead, clxxxii, 25.

13. The teacher . . . stands in the centre of the way, and those who can follow him.

Mencius, xiii, 43.

14. Of whatsoever teachings thou canst assure thyself that they conduce to dispassion and not to passion, to detachment and not to bondage, etc. . . . of such teachings thou mayest with certainty affirm: This is the Master's message.

THE BUDDHA. *Vinaya, Mahavagga*, ii, 10.

15. So long as a Tathagata, a Buddha, arises not there is no shining forth of great light. . . . But as soon as a Tathagata arises all these things take place, and then there is a proclaiming, a teaching, a showing forth.

THE BUDDHA. *Samyutta-Nikaya*, v, 442.

16. Who travelled to the lofty heights above us, who searches out and shows the path to many.

Rig Veda, x, 14, 1.

17. Thus I am born . . . for the establishment of righteousness.

KRISHNA. *Bhagavad-Gita*, iv, 8.

52

The Inner Teaching

1. Unto you it is given to know the mystery of the kingdom of God: but unto them that are without, all these things are done in parables.

JESUS.   *Mark* iv, 11.

2. When they were alone, he expounded all things to his disciples.

Mark iv, 34.

3. But strong meat belongeth to them that are of full age, even those who by reason of use have their senses exercised to discern both good and evil.

PAUL.   *Hebrews* v, 14.

4. The secret things belong unto the Lord our God: but those things which are revealed belong unto us and to our children for ever, that we may do all the words of this law.

Deuteronomy xxix, 29.

5. Their vestments be knowingly and skilfully worked with various feathers ... in which, ... they say, is contained certain divine mysteries.

SIR THOMAS MORE.   *Utopia,* Book II.

6. My dark and cloudy words, they do but hold the truth, as cabinets enclose the gold.

JOHN BUNYAN.   *Pilgrim's Progress (Introduction).*

7. Now, said he, compare this hen to your King, and these chickens to his obedient ones ... he has also a brooding voice, for them that are under his wing.

JOHN BUNYAN. *Pilgrim's Progress*, Part 2.

8. Reader, may so thy eyes with truth be lit,
   They pierce the meaning hid within this book.

DANTE. *Purgatorio*, viii, 4.

9. Mysteries ... are the secret things which can neither be taught nor sold publicly, which can be only acquired by a heart that has attained to wisdom and love.

ECKARTSHAUSEN. *The Cloud upon the Sanctuary*, iii.

10. Those of the Light need not the mysteries, because they are light being purified; but the race of mankind, they are those who need them.

Pistis Sophia (p. 231 *a*, *Coptic MS.*).

11. He who is perfected in baptism, and initiated into the lesser mysteries, becomes ripe for the greater mysteries, for the Gnosis, or scientific knowledge of God.

CLEMENT OF ALEXANDRIA.

12. That these certain doctrines, not made known to the multitude, are revealed after the exoteric ones have been taught, is not a peculiarity of Christianity alone, but also of philosophic systems, in which certain truths are exoteric and others esoteric.

ORIGEN. *Contra Celsum*, i, 7.

13. Whoever penetrates and analyses these speeches will discover that they are the only speeches with meaning, that they are the most inspired.

PLATO. *The Symposium* (222).

14. The skilful masters in old times, with a subtle and exquisite penetration, comprehended its mysteries, and were deep so as to elude men's knowledge.

LAO TSE. *Tao Teh King*, xv.

15. The Way of the true man is widely apparent and yet hidden. Thus the ordinary man and woman, ignorant though they are, can yet have some knowledge of it; and yet in its perfection even a sage finds that there is something there which he does not know.

TZU SSU. *The Doctrine of the Mean*, 12.

16. This gentle lord gives wisdom to the simple; the wiser god leads on the wise to riches.

Rig Veda, vii, 86, 7.

17. I will open unto you, whose heart rejects not, the most profound knowledge . . . the deepest mystery.

KRISHNA. *Bhagavad-Gita*, ix, 1.

53

Refraining from Speaking to the Unreceptive

1. Give not that which is holy unto the dogs, neither cast ye your pearls before swine.

JESUS.   *Matthew* vii, 6.

2. Speak not in the ears of a fool: for he will despise the wisdom of thy words.

Proverbs xxiii, 9.

3. For few could understand what they said; they naturally spoke the language of Canaan, but they that kept the fair were the men of this world.

JOHN BUNYAN.   *Pilgrim's Progress*, Part 1.

4. The people at large were not capable of comprehending high interior truth, and the danger would have been too great in confiding that which was of all most holy to incapable people.

ECKARTSHAUSEN.   *The Cloud upon the Sanctuary*, ii.

5. Our Lord and Teacher charged us saying, "Ye shall keep my mysteries for me and for the sons of mine house."

Clementine Homilies, xix, 20.

6. We conceal and pass by in silence the truths of deeper import when we see that our audience is composed of simpler minds, which need such instruction as is figuratively termed "milk."

ORIGEN. *Contra Celsum,* iii, 52.

7. While you were younger . . . the god did not permit me to discourse with you, lest my discourse should be in vain.

PLATO. *The First Alcibiades.*

8. The mandate of the mysteries orders that they shall not be divulged to those who are uninitiated. For as that which is divine cannot be unfolded to the multitude, this mandate forbids the attempt to elucidate it to anyone but him who is fortunately able to perceive it.

PLOTINUS. *Ennead,* vi, 9, 11.

9. It is not safe to speak of God with those who are corrupted by false opinion.

PORPHYRY. *Letter to Marcella,* xv.

10. Keep silence, thou who art admitted to the secret rites.

Chaldean Oracles (Kroll 55).

11. Let none who is outside know; it is a mystery, and the ignorant know it not.

The Egyptian Book of the Dead, clxi (Rubric).

12. It is better to withhold than to fill to overflowing.

LAO TSE. *Tao Teh King,* ix.

13. He who knows, does not speak; he who speaks, does not know.

LAO TSE.   *Tao Teh King*, lvi.

14. Those who excel in beauty become vain; those who excel in strength become violent. To such, it is useless to speak of Tao.

LIEH TSE.

15. When that which is given out from the mind in possession of it, is not received by the mind without, the sage will not give it out.

Kwang Tse, xiv, 5.

16. You cannot speak of the ocean to a well-frog. A small bag cannot be made to contain what is large.

Kwang Tse, xvii, 1; xviii, 5.

17. . . . yet I did not reveal them. I might have revealed it, and others would not have believed it. Now, had they not believed me, it would have been to their loss and sorrow.

THE BUDDHA.   *Samyutta-Nikaya*, ii, 261.

18. This profoundest mystery one should not mention to anyone who is not a son, or who is not a pupil, or who is not tranquil. However to one who is devoted to none other, or to one who is supplied with all the qualifications, one may give it.

Maitri Upanishad, vi, 29.

19. A teacher of the Veda should die with his knowledge rather than sow it on barren soil.

Laws of Manu, ii, 113.

20. I am not known to evil-doers, nor to foolish ones, nor to the base and churlish; nor to those whose mind is cheated by the show of things.

KRISHNA. *Bhagavad-Gita*, vii, 15.

54

The Narrow Way

1. Strait is the gate, and narrow is the way, which leadeth unto life, and few there be that find it.

JESUS. *Matthew* vii, 14.

2. They who would see Me and reach My kingdom need must attain Me with pain and suffering.

Extra-canonical Saying of Jesus.

3. It is as straight as a rule can make it. This is the way thou must go.

JOHN BUNYAN. *Pilgrim's Progress*, Part 1.

4. I, as a priest, would learn the straight path by Righteousness.

ZARATHUSHTRA. *The Avesta, Yasna*, xxxiii, 6.

5. Great Tao is very straight; but the people love by-ways.

LAO TSE. *Tao Teh King*, liii.

6. Like a whetstone is the Chou way;
   Straight as an arrow!

Mencius, x, 7.

7. This Reality that I have reached is profound, hard to see, hard to understand . . . beyond the sphere of thinking, subtle, to be penetrated by the wise alone.

THE BUDDHA. *Vinaya-Pitaka*, i, 4.

8. Difficult is the hearing of the True Law, difficult is the birth of the Awakened.

Dhammapada, 182.

9. Very narrow is the way like the edge of a sword.

Nanak, i, 363 *(Sikhism)*.

10. The ancient narrow path that stretches far away has been touched by me, has been found by me. By it the wise, the knowers of Brahma, go up hence to the heavenly world, released.

Brihad-aranyaka Upanishad, iv, 4, 8.

11. The sharp edge of a razor, hard to traverse, a difficult path is this—thus the wise say.

Katha Upanishad, iii, 14.

12. Hard the travail is for such as bend their minds to reach th'Unmanifest. That viewless path shall scarce be trod by man bearing the flesh.

KRISHNA. *Bhagavad-Gita*, xii, 5.

55

The Master's Authority

1. Though I bear record of myself, yet my record is true: for I know whence I came and whither I go.

JESUS.   *John* viii, 14.

2. I and my Father are one.

JESUS.   *John* x, 30.

3. Jesus said unto him, I am the way, the truth, and the life: no man cometh unto the Father but by me.

John xiv, 6.

4. Christ the same yesterday, and to-day, and for ever.

PAUL.   *Hebrews* xiii, 8.

5. I certify you, brethren, that the gospel which was preached of me is not after man. For I neither received it of man, neither was I taught it, but by revelation of Jesus Christ.

PAUL.   *Galatians* i, 11.

6. The Lord spake unto Moses face to face, as a man speaketh unto his friend.

Exodus xxxiii, 11.

7. Yet have I more to say . . . for I am filled as the moon at full.

Ecclesiasticus xxxix, 12.

8. In this land the Shining Ones commonly walked, because it was upon the borders of heaven . . . and the gardener said, even to me . . .

JOHN BUNYAN.   Pilgrim's Progress, Part 1.

9. What we teach is not the result of opinion and speculation, but of actual experience.

PARACELSUS.   De Generatio Hominis.

10. All that I am now saying is not hyperphysical extravagance; it is reality, absolute truth. . . . Absolute truth exists only for interior and spiritual man who possesses . . . an interior organ to receive the absolute truth of the transcendental world, a spiritual faculty which cognizes spiritual objects as objectively and naturally as the exterior senses perceive external phenomena.

ECKARTSHAUSEN.   The Cloud upon the Sanctuary.

11. Divination, which is the art of communion between gods and men.

PLATO.   The Symposium (188).

12. Whoever becomes one by mingling with deity, and afterwards recollects this union, will have with himself an image of it.

PLOTINUS.   Ennead, vi, 9, 11.

13. Look thou to My Face and turn from all save Me; for My Authority is eternal and shall never cease; My Kingdom is lasting and shall not be overthrown.

BAHA-U-LLAH.   Of Divine Humanity.

14. I will proclaim the word which the Most Beneficent spoke to me.

ZARATHUSHTRA. *The Avesta, Yasna*, xlv, 5.

15. I am Yesterday, To-day, and To-morrow.

The Egyptian Book of the Dead, lxiv, 2.

16. My words come from one Source.

LAO TSE. *Tao Teh King*, lxx.

17. I, brethren, am one that is skilled in this world, and skilled in the world beyond; in Mara's realm, and in that beyond; in the realm of death, and that beyond death.

THE BUDDHA. *Majjhima-Nikaya*, i, 34.

18. He is the brahmin indeed who knows his former lives, and who knows heaven and hell.

Dhammapada, 423.

19. Many are the births that I have passed through, and . . . all mine I know.

KRISHNA. *Bhagavad-Gita*, iv, 5.

20. I am the Way, the Fosterer, the Lord, the Witness.

KRISHNA. *Bhagavad-Gita*, ix, 18.

56

Knowledge of the Kingdom of Heaven

---

1. When he, the Spirit of truth, is come, he shall guide you into all truth.

JESUS.   John xvi, 13.

2. He shall baptize you with the Holy Ghost, and with fire.

Matthew iii, 11.

3. . . . cloven tongues like as of fire, and . . . they were all filled with the Holy Ghost.

Acts ii, 3.

4. We speak wisdom among the perfect. . . . Unto us God has revealed it through the Spirit.

PAUL.   1 Corinthians ii, 6–10 (R.V.).

5. How can anyone teach Christ if he does not know Him? Can that which is not eternal know the eternal?

PARACELSUS.   Liber Philosophiae.

6. The science of the prophets was experimental possession of the truth of the symbols. The highest degree (for successive development to higher altitudes) is the entire opening of our inner sensorium, by which the inner man attains the objective vision of real and metaphysical verities.

ECKARTSHAUSEN.   The Cloud upon the Sanctuary, ii.

7. By fire we perceive the Unseen Fire.

EMPEDOCLES.

8. Only he who perceives Beauty with the eye of his soul can bring forth veritable Virtue and not its image. For it is not the image but the truth that he grasps.

PLATO. *The Symposium* (212).

9. He who desires the light of knowledge desires the gift of a priest of fire.

The Avesta, Yasht, liii.

10. For if the mortal draw nigh to the Fire, he shall have Light from God.

Chaldean Oracles (Kroll 53).

11. The iron which is the ceiling of heaven openeth itself before Pepi, and he passeth through it.

The Pyramid of King Pepi 1st, 169.

12. Knowledge of the Eternal is illumination.

LAO TSE. *Tao Teh King,* lv.

13. He [Agni] shall bring hitherward the gods.

Rig Veda, i, 25, 10.

14. Thou, Agni, art our thread and bridge; thou art the path leading to the gods.

Taittiriya Brahmana, ii, 4, 2, 6.

Evolution and Attainment

57

In Everything is Spirit and Law in Operation

1. Raise the stone, and thou shalt find me; cleave the wood, and there am I.

> *Extra-canonical Saying of Jesus (Oxyrhynchus papyrus, i, 10).*

2. Whither shall I go from thy spirit?

> *Psalm* cxxxix, 7.

3. Thine incorruptible spirit is in all things.

> *Wisdom of Solomon* xii, 1.

4. No man should conceive so vile and base an opinion of the dignity of man's nature, as to think . . . that the world runneth by chance governed by no divine providence.

> SIR THOMAS MORE.   *Utopia*, Book II.

5. There exists nothing in which is not a hidden principle of life.

> PARACELSUS.

6. As above, so below; as below, so above.

> *Saying of the Medieval Alchemists.*

7. I saw how his omnipotence penetrated everything, and was the foundation of all things; all that befell in the whole wide world was according to His will.

> KOMENSKY.   *The Labyrinth*, xlii, 5.

8. And what other name can we give to it but primal being? 'Tis it alone that acts and suffers becoming all for all, through all eternal Deity, deprived and wronged of its own self by names and forms.

APOLLONIUS OF TYANA.   *To Valerius.*

9. Thou shalt know how, by divine law, nature is in everything alike.

Golden Verses of the Pythagoreans, 52.

10. The sensible fire is in everything, and passes through everything unmingled, and springs from all, and whilst all-luminous, is hidden, unknown, in its essential nature.

DIONYSIUS THE AREOPAGITE.

11. Our forefathers,—better men than ourselves, and in closer converse with the gods,—have handed down to us this tradition, that all things which are said by us to be, are composed of both One and Many.

PLATO.   *Philebus* (16, *c*).

12. Zeus, ruler of Nature, that governest all things with law.

CLEANTHES.   *Hymn to Zeus.*

13. Generally, above and below, thou shalt find but the same things. For all things throughout, there is but one and the same order; one and the same God, the same substance and the same law.

MARCUS AURELIUS.   *Meditations,* vii, 1 & 6.

14. The One is not absent from any thing, and yet is separated from all things.

PLOTINUS.   *Ennead*, vi, 9, 4.

15. Reason tells us that the Divine is present everywhere and in all men.

PORPHYRY.   *Letter to Marcella*, xi.

16. All things have for their Father the one Fire.

Chaldean Oracles (*Kroll* 15).

17. All-pervading is the Great Tao.

LAO TSE.   *Tao Teh King*, xxxiv.

18. I see that nothing proceeds without method and order. The Tao is to be found complete and diffused in all things.

Kwang Tse, xi, 5; xiii, 9.

19. It stands pervading everything in the world. The being of great power is stationed in the heart of all.

Anugita, xxv.

20. Behold but one in all things.

Kabir, ii, 320 (*Sikhism*).

21. Varuna, true to holy law, sits down among his people; he, most wise, sits there to govern all.

Rig Veda, i, 25, 10.

22. What is here, the same is there; and what is there, the same is here.

Katha Upanishad, ii, 4, 10.

23. For truly, everything here is Brahma.

Mandukya Upanishad, 2.

24. Let him recognize the subtle nature of the supreme Soul, and its presence in all things, both the highest and the lowest.

Laws of Manu, vi, 65.

25. One pervading Spirit's stress, one Force in every place, though manifold.

KRISHNA.   *Bhagavad-Gita*, ix, 15.

26. The Father of Life, of existence—through whom all acts and breathes . . . whose wisdom has meditated the excellence of all that exists.

The Popol Vuh, i, 1.

58

Gradual and Inevitable Progress

1. Blessed are the poor in spirit: for theirs is the kingdom of heaven.

JESUS.   *Matthew* v, 3.

2. Force not the course of the river.

Ecclesiasticus iv, 26.

3. By slow degrees new truth would meet my view.

DANTE.   *Paradiso*, xxxiii, 12.

4. Light, especially the celestial light (and this is to be well noted), must not be suddenly presented in its full radiance (lest we be completely blinded and hardened in our ignorance), but gradually introduced. For men must be raised by slow stages ... we must make a beginning with the things which they know and slowly lead them to what they do not know.

KOMENSKY.   *The Way of Light*, xii, 13.

5. By the perception of the outer, which is the symbol of the interior, [men may] by degrees be enabled safely to approach the interior spiritual truths. ... The Kingdom of God ... spreads itself gradually.

ECKARTSHAUSEN.   *The Cloud upon the Sanctuary*, ii & vi.

6. Who is there that can make muddy water clear? But if allowed to remain still, it will gradually become clear of itself.

LAO TSE. *Tao Teh King*, xv.

7. The characteristic of Tao is gentleness.

LAO TSE. *Tao Teh King*, xl.

8. The method of spontaneity proceeds in stillness. The method of heaven and earth proceeds gently and gradually.

Yin Fu King, iii, 6.

9. Slow is the arising of mindfulness.

Anguttara-Nikaya, Tetrads, 186.

10. Just as the mighty ocean deepens and slopes gradually down, . . . even so, progress is gradual.

THE BUDDHA. *Udana*, v, 5.

59

All Will Eventually Attain

1. The crooked shall become straight, and the rough ways smooth; and all flesh shall see the salvation of God.

JOHN THE BAPTIST. *Luke* iii, 5–6 (R.*V.*).

2. God willeth that all should receive of His gifts.

Extra-canonical Saying of Jesus.

3. This corruptible must put on incorruption, and this mortal must put on immortality.

PAUL. 1 *Corinthians* xv, 53.

4. All the ends of the earth shall see the salvation of our God.

Isaiah lii, 10.

5. There will be no transgression which will not be set right, no displeasure which will not be forgiven, no anger that will not be pacified. There can be nothing that shall not be known, no loss of anything beloved that shall not be regained, no end to the Gwynvyd that shall be attained.

Welsh Triad.

6. All men are called, the called may be chosen, if they become ripe for entrance. . . . The love and spirit of God will one day alone vivify all humanity.

ECKARTSHAUSEN. *The Cloud upon the Sanctuary,* ii & vi.

7. Thus dost Thou harmonize into One all good and evil things, that there should be one everlasting Reason of them all.

CLEANTHES.   *Hymn to Zeus.*

8. ... that in the Kingdom ye [Mazda] may bring all creatures to perfection through good thought.

ZARATHUSHTRA.   *The Avesta, Yasna,* xxxiv, 3.

9. Thou shouldst not consider even anyone hopeless of heaven.

Shayast-na-shayast, xii, 28 (*Zoroastrianism*).

10. That which is incomplete shall become complete.

LAO TSE.   *Tao Teh King,* xxii.

11. It is the characteristic of Heaven to be the real. It is the characteristic of man to be coming-to-be-real.

TZU SSU.   *The Doctrine of the Mean,* vii.

12. The tendency of man's nature to good is like the tendency of water to flow downwards. There are none but have this tendency to good, just as all water flows downwards.

Mencius, vi, 1, 2.

13. From the Son of Heaven down to the common people there is unity in this: that for everybody the bringing of the individual self to flower is to be taken as the root.

The Great Learning, 1 (*Chinese*).

14. Open to all be the gates of deathlessness.

THE BUDDHA.   *Vinaya, Mahavagga,* i, 5, 12.

15. Two paths, I've heard—the one that leads to the fathers, and one that leads to gods—belong to mortals. By these two, every moving thing here travels.

Brihad-aranyaka Upanishad, vi, 2, 2.

16. All men everywhere shall fall into my path.

KRISHNA. *Bhagavad-Gita*, iv, 11.

17. Many roads thou hast fashioned—all of them lead to the Light.

KIPLING. *A Song to Mithras* (from *Puck of Pook's Hill*).

18. What We have created and fashioned will attain its fulfilment.

The Popol Vuh, i, 1.

60

Brotherhood; Love

1. Whosoever shall do the will of my Father which is in Heaven, the same is my brother, and sister, and mother.

JESUS.   *Matthew* xii, 50.

2. He that loveth another hath fulfilled the law.

PAUL.   *Romans* xiii, 8.

3. Love suffereth long and is kind; . . . is not provoked, taketh not account of evil; rejoiceth not in unrighteousness, but rejoiceth with the truth.

PAUL.   1 *Corinthians* xiii, 4–7 (R.*V.*).

4. Have we not all one father?

Malachi ii, 10.

5. It is the nature of light to spread itself, indeed, it is the nature of every good thing to communicate itself.

KOMENSKY.   *The Way of Light,* xxi, 22.

6. He who may be chosen by God is as the first; he presents himself among the others without presumption, he is received by them without jealousy. . . . He who is ripe is joined to the chain, perhaps often where he thought least likely, and at a point of which he knew nothing himself.

ECKARTSHAUSEN.   *The Cloud upon the Sanctuary,* ii.

7. Love never injures, nor is ever injured by, god or man; for though he suffer it is not by violence, for upon Love violence lays no hand; nor when he acts does he act violently.

PLATO.   *The Symposium* (196).

8. Zeus hath so formed the nature of the reasoning creature that he may never win aught of his own good without he furnish something of service to the common good.

EPICTETUS.   *Dissertations,* i, 19.

9. Everything [there] is in itself, not locally, and each is united to each, and is at the same time separate from each.

PLOTINUS.   *Ennead,* iv, 3, 11.

10. Ye are all the fruits of one tree and the leaves of one branch. Walk, then, with perfect charity, concord, affection and agreement.

BAHA-U-LLAH.

11. What is the Will of Heaven like? The answer is "To love all men everywhere alike."

Mo Tse, xxviii.

12. Only a loving man can serve the small when he is great; only a wise man can serve the great when he is small.

Mencius, ii, 3.

13. He that has found the way has many helpers.

Mencius, iv, 1.

14. Where there is sympathy, there will not be separation.

Kwang Tse, xx, 5.

15. Whosoever lives according to the doctrine, he is very near to me.

THE BUDDHA.

16. Let a man cultivate good will towards all the world.

Sutta-Nipata, i, 8, 8.

17. Those who are helpmates to all; those who are a sanctuary to all; those men are in the way of heaven.

Hitopadesa, i, 4.

61

Safe-keeping

1. Are not two sparrows sold for a farthing? and one of them shall not fall on the ground without your Father. But the very hairs of your head are all numbered. Fear not therefore, ye are of more value than many sparrows.

JESUS.   *Matthew* x, 29–31.

2. Where two or three are gathered together in my name, there am I in the midst of them.

JESUS.   *Matthew* xviii, 20.

3. He hath said, I will never leave thee, nor forsake thee.

PAUL.   *Hebrews* xiii, 5.

4. He shall give his angels charge over thee, to keep thee in all thy ways. They shall bear thee up in their hands, lest thou dash thy foot against a stone.

Psalm xci, 11.

5. But the righteous live for ever, and in the Lord is their reward, and the care for them with the Most High . . . with his right hand shall he cover them, and with his arm shall he shield them.

Wisdom of Solomon v, 15–16.

6. I have a key in my bosom, called Promise, that will, I am persuaded, open any lock in Doubting Castle.

JOHN BUNYAN.   *Pilgrim's Progress*, Part 1.

7. Thou knowest the appointed end of all things, and all the paths thereto: all the leaves that earth puts forth in spring, and the number of grains of sand. . . . Surely the great mind of Zeus pilots the destiny of those whom he loves.

PINDAR.

8. God has forethought for all things, and there exist angels, divine and good spirits, who behold all that is done, and from whose notice there is no escape.

PORPHYRY. *Letter to Marcella*, xxi.

9. I am he who protecteth you for millions of years.

The Egyptian Book of the Dead, xlii, 19.

10. Put thou thyself for safe-keeping in the hand of the Almighty.

The Teaching of Amen-em-apt, 253.

11. To fear the power of heaven is protection everlasting.

Mencius, i, 2, 3.

12. May we be in thy keeping, O thou leader, wide-ruling Varuna.

Rig Veda, ii, 28, 3.

13. Those who worship me with devotion are in me, and I also am in them.

KRISHNA. *Bhagavad-Gita*, ix, 29.

62

Prayer

1. When thou prayest, enter into thine inner chamber, and having shut thy door, pray to thy Father which is in secret.

JESUS.   *Matthew* vi, 6 (R.*V.*).

2. And being in an agony he prayed more earnestly: and his sweat was as it were great drops of blood falling down to the ground.

Luke xxii, 44.

3. The effectual fervent prayer of a righteous man availeth much.

James v, 16.

4. The Lord heareth the prayer of the righteous.

Proverbs xv, 29.

5. The prayer of the humble pierceth the clouds.

Ecclesiasticus xxxv, 17.

6. It is not always necessary to grant things not asked for, lest, by so doing, they become of little esteem; but when the want of a thing is felt, it then comes under, in the eyes of him that feels it, that estimate that properly is its due, and so, consequently, will be thereafter used.

JOHN BUNYAN.   *Pilgrim's Progress*, Part 2.

7. Either the gods have power to assist us, or they have not. If they have not, what does praying to them signify? If they have, why do you not rather pray that they would remove your desires than satisfy them, and rather set you above fear than keep away the thing you are afraid of?

MARCUS AURELIUS.   *Meditations,* ix, 40.

8. We must ask of God only such gifts as are worthy of God,—that is to say such things as we cannot obtain from any except God.

PORPHYRY.   *Letter to Marcella,* xi.

9. Prayer attains the effect by a community of feeling betwixt certain parts of the universe, which lie as it were along the same stretched-out cord, so that if the cord be twitched at its lower extremity the tremor is felt above.

PLOTINUS.   *Ennead,* iv, 4, 40.

10. Invoking God himself, not with external speech, but with the soul itself, extending ourselves in prayer to him, since we shall then be able to pray to him properly, when we approach by ourselves alone to the alone.

PLOTINUS.   *Ennead,* v, 1, 6.

11. Mazda will hear those who are bent on increasing good.

ZARATHUSHTRA.   *The Avesta, Yasna,* xlv, 6.

12. If you call me by day or by night by these names, I will come to assist and help you, the angel Sraosha will then come to assist and help you and the spirits . . . will come to assist you.

The Avesta, Yasht, i.

13. Behold the charm is given to me, from wherever it is, swifter than greyhounds and quicker than light.

The Egyptian Book of the Dead, xxiv, 3.

14. The prayer of the long-suffering man is greater than force.

The Teaching of Ptah-hotep, xx.

15. When they weep he hearkens to their cry.

The Teaching of King Khati, 135.

16. Devoting thy mind one-pointedly . . . pray.

The Tibetan Book of the Dead, i, 2.

17. My nearest, closest armour is prayer.

Rig Veda, vi, 75, 19.

18. May they who have attained the life of spirits, gentle and righteous, aid us when we call them.

Rig Veda, x, 15, 1.

63

My Father's House

1. In my Father's house are many mansions.

Jesus. *John* xiv, 2.

2. We have a building of God, an house not made with hands, eternal in the heavens.

Paul. *2 Corinthians* v, 1.

3. For ye are not come unto the mount that might be touched, and that burned with fire, nor unto blackness, and darkness, and tempest. . . . But ye are come unto mount Sion, and unto the city of the living God, the heavenly Jerusalem, and to an innumerable company of angels.

Paul. *Hebrews* xii, 18–22.

4. He set me upon a very high mountain . . . and brought me to the temple.

Ezekiel xl, xli, etc.

5. The holy tabernacle, which thou hast prepared from the beginning.

Wisdom of Solomon ix, 8.

6. He lift up his eyes, and behold there was a very stately palace before him, the name of which was Beautiful.

John Bunyan. *Pilgrim's Progress*, Part 1.

7. ... the interior Church. This community of light has existed since the first day of the world's creation, and its duration will be to the end of time. It ... possesses a School, in which all who thirst for knowledge are instructed by the Spirit of Wisdom itself; and all the mysteries of God and of nature are preserved therein for the children of light.

ECKARTSHAUSEN.   *The Cloud upon the Sanctuary,* ii.

8. The subjects which are taught and learned in this [Hyperphysical] School are such as the eye of no man has ever seen, nor ear heard, nor do they come into the heart of men, but God alone reveals them through his Spirit.

KOMENSKY.   *The Way of Light, Dedication,* 18.

9. There are many ravishing views and opening paths within the bounds of heaven, whereon the blessed family of the gods go to and fro, each in performance of his own proper work; and they are followed by all who from time to time possess both will and power, for envy has no place in the celestial choir.

PLATO.   *Phaedrus* (247).

10. All perfect things are garnered up in the splendid residence of Mazda.

ZARATHUSHTRA.   *The Avesta, Yasna,* xxx, 10.

11. He [the archangel Sraosha] who has a palace with a thousand pillars erected on the highest summit of the celestial mountain. It has its own light from inside, and from outside is decorated with stars.

The Avesta, Yasna, lvii, 21.

12. For him [Mithra] the lord Mazda himself reared a palace on the celestial mountain where is no night, nor darkness, no cold wind, nor hot, no smoke, nor fog, nor any putrefaction.

The Avesta, Yasht, x, 50.

13. In the celestial mansions of heaven which my divine Father Tem hath stablished, let my hands lay hold upon the wheat.

The Egyptian Book of the Dead, lxxii.

14. Varuna, thou glorious lord, I have entered thy lofty house, thine house with its thousand portals.... Bring me to dwell in that abiding city.

Rig Veda, vii, 88, 5–7.

64

Eternal Wisdom

1. The hidden wisdom, which God ordained before the world.

PAUL.   1 *Corinthians* ii, 7.

2. The faithful and true witness, the beginning of the creation of God.

Revelation iii, 14.

3. The light that cometh from her [Wisdom] never goeth out.

Wisdom of Solomon vii, 10.

4. Wisdom cometh from the Lord, and is with him for ever. . . . Wisdom hath been created before all things.

Ecclesiasticus i, 1–4.

5. Wisdom . . . the pure substance out of which all has been made.

ECKARTSHAUSEN.   *The Cloud upon the Sanctuary*, v.

6. Wisdom was generated before any beginning that can be either comprehended or expressed.

ORIGEN.   *De Principiis*, i, ii, 2.

7. Wisdom, in whose assurance Thou governest all things with justice.

CLEANTHES.   *Hymn to Zeus.*

8. Now Maät is the foundation of the Almighty.

The Teaching of Amen-em-apt, 409.

9. He who created by means of his wisdom.

ZARATHUSHTRA. *The Avesta, Yasna*, xlviii, 4.

10. How deep and unfathomable Tao is. It appears to be Ancestor of all things.

LAO TSE. *Tao Teh King*, iv.

11. Before there were heaven and earth, from of old, there Tao was, securely existing.

Kwang Tse, vi, 7.

12. In whom all wisdom centres, as the nave is set within the wheel.

Rig Veda, viii, 41, 6.

13. Without beginning thou embracest all, for by thee are all the worlds created.

Svetasvatara Upanishad, iv, 4.

14. Older than eld, Who stored the worlds with wealth of life. . . . Who wottest all, and art Wisdom Thyself.

Bhagavad-Gita, xi, 38.

15. The Creator, the Fashioner, the Dominator, the Serpent Covered with Feathers.

The Popol Vuh, i, 1.

65

Beginnings

1. In the beginning was the Word, and the Word was with God, and the Word was God. The same was in the beginning with God.

John i, 1.

2. And God said, Let us make man in our image.

Genesis i, 26.

3. The Lord possessed me [Wisdom] in the beginning of his way, before his works of old. I was set up from ever-lasting, from the beginning, or ever the earth was ... when he marked out the foundation of the earth: then I was by him, as a master workman.

Proverbs viii, 22–30 (R.*V*.).

4. As, after its destruction, there will be another world, so also we believe that others existed before the present came into being.

ORIGEN. *De Principiis*, 3, v, 3.

5. This universe is generated. Again, with reference to what exists, it must necessarily have arisen from some cause.

PLATO. *Timaeus*, ix.

6. If a beginning were created from anything it would not be a beginning.

PLATO. *Phaedrus* (245).

7. He [Mazda] first created by means of his own light.

ZARATHUSHTRA. *The Avesta, Yasna,* xxxi, 7.

8. The Father caused to swell forth seven firmaments of worlds.

Chaldean Oracles (Kroll 31).

9. Thou art the god One who came into being in the beginning of time. Thou didst create the earth, thou didst fashion man. . . . Homage to thee, who dost rest upon Maät.

Hymn to Ra, Papyrus of Hu-nefer.

10. Men and women are the images of Him.

The Teaching of King Khati, xxviii.

11. There was something, undefined and complete, coming into existence before Heaven and Earth. How still it was and formless, standing alone and undergoing no change, reaching everywhere and in no danger of being exhausted. It may be regarded as the Mother of all things!

LAO TSE. *Tao Teh King,* xxv.

12. All things under Heaven sprang from Tao as existing; that existence sprang from Tao as non-existent.

LAO TSE. *Tao Teh King,* xl.

13. There is a creative principle which is itself uncreated; there is a principle of change which is itself unchanging. The uncreated is able to create life; the unchanging is able to effect change. That which is produced cannot but

continue producing; that which is evolved cannot but continue evolving. Hence there is constant production and constant evolution.

Lieh Tse, i.

14. There was a beginning. There was a beginning before that beginning. There was a beginning previous to that beginning before there was the beginning.

Kwang Tse, ii, 6.

15. In the Great Beginning there was nothing; nothing that could be named. In this state arose the first existence, but without concrete form; and from this things could then be produced. This can be described as spiritual power at work. The formless then came to be divided.

Kwang Tse, xii, 8.

16. There is no coming-into-existence without destruction; there is no destruction devoid of origination; neither origination nor destruction can truly be without stability.

Pravacana-sara, ii, 8 (*Jainism*).

17. Existence, in the earliest age of gods, from non-existence sprang.

Rig Veda, x, 72, 3.

18. The entire universe has been created by Brahma.

Taittiriya Brahmana, iii, 12, 9, 2.

19. Verily, in the beginning this world was Brahma.

Brihad-aranyaka Upanishad, i, 4, 10.

20. In the beginning this world was just Being, one only, without a second. . . . It bethought itself: "Would that I were many. Let me procreate myself."

Chandogya Upanishad, vi, 2, 1.

21. At the advent of Brahma's day all manifested things are produced from the unmanifested.

KRISHNA. *Bhagavad-Gita*, viii, 18.

22. Nature and the Spirit both have no beginning.

KRISHNA. *Bhagavad-Gita*, xiii, 20.

23. The source of the existent and the non-existent is but one.

Sanatsugativa, vi, 15.

24. All was in suspense, all was calm and silent, all was motionless, all was peaceful, and empty was the immensity of the heavens. Behold then the first word. . . . Then his word came here with the Dominator and the Serpent covered with blue and green. . . . "Earth," they said; and on the instant it was formed.

The Popol Vuh, i, 1.

14. The immortality, which I have obtained by deeds, words and offerings, and purity, I give to thee, O Mazda.

ZARATHUSHTRA.   *The Avesta, Yasna*, xxxiv, 1.

15. Verily they ask, saying, what is the end, and the answer is, the return to the beginning.

Gulshan-i-Raz (Sufism).

16. The path of Tao is a return to the Source.

LAO TSE.   *Tao Teh King*, xl.

17. Realness is self-completing, and the way of it is to be self-directing.

TZU SSU.   *The Doctrine of the Mean*, 25.

18. The course of evolution ends where it started, without a beginning; it finishes up where it began, in Not-Being.

LIEH TSE.

19. It was separation that led to completion.

Kwang Tse, ii, 4.

20. When a thing's nature has been developed to the full, there is a return to its spiritual character; and when this has been fully attained, it is the same as in the very beginning.

Kwang Tse, xii, 8.

21. When self-mastery is attained, then all things are in a state of completeness.

HUAI NAN TSE.   *Yuen Tao Huin*, xxi.

22. Let one worship It as that from which he came forth, as that into which he will be dissolved.

Chandogya Upanishad, iii, 14, 1.

23. All the worlds, even the realm of Brahma, are subject to return; but after attaining Me there is no rebirth.

KRISHNA. *Bhagavad-Gita*, viii, 16.

24. I am the beginning, the middle, and also the end of all beings.

KRISHNA. *Bhagavad-Gita*, x, 20.

67

The Attainment of Freedom from Rebirth

1. Peace in heaven.

Luke xix, 38.

2. Blessed are the pure in heart: for they shall see God.

JESUS.　*Matthew* v, 8.

3. Let not him who seeketh cease until he findeth; and when he findeth he shall wonder; wondering he shall enter the kingdom; entering the kingdom he shall be at peace.

Extra-canonical Saying of Jesus (*Oxyrhynchus Papyrus*, 654, 1).

4. I have suffered the loss of all things ... if by any means I might attain unto the resurrection of the dead.

PAUL.　*Philippians* iii, 8–11.

5. Now no more to return to corruption.

PAUL.　*Acts* xiii, 34.

6. Mark the perfect man, and behold the upright: for the end of that man is peace.

Psalm xxxvii, 37.

7. In respect of progress towards perfection, ... ultimately we become creatures like the Creator, set free

from the dominion of creatures and of self, and restored
to God our source and to a blessed peace in him.

KOMENSKY. *The Way of Light, Dedication*, 20.

8. To God again the enfranchised soul must tend; He is
her home, her Author and her end. No death is hers;
when earthly eyes grow dim starlike she soars and
Godlike melts in him.

VIRGIL.

9. Ye have been in great afflictions and great tribulations,
in your pourings into different bodies in this world. And
after all these afflictions which came from yourselves, ye
have struggled and fought . . . until ye found all the
mysteries of the Kingdom of Light, which have purified
you, and transformed you into refined light, most pure, and
ye have become pure light itself.

The Pistis Sophia (p. 230 *a, Coptic MS.*).

10. . . . the possibility of attaining to perfection being
granted to man at the beginning through the dignity of
the divine image, and the perfect realization of the divine
likeness being reached in the end by the fulfilment of the
necessary works.

ORIGEN. *De Principiis*, 3, vi, 1.

11. Having established noblest reason as a charioteer,
from on high, and when, having put aside thy body, thou
comest into the free aether, thou shalt be deathless, a god
imperishable, no longer mortal.

Golden Verses of the Pythagoreans, 69–71.

12. I shall go soaring to the firmament of heaven, to be made one with Zeus.

EURIPIDES.

13. For whoever is initiated thus far . . . there bursts that Beauty which is marvellous; and for this end were all our former labours. It is everlasting and is neither begotten nor perishable, and never waxes and never wanes.

PLATO. *The Symposium* (210).

14. Virtue proceeding to the end, and being ingenerated in the soul in conjunction with wisdom, will present God to the view.

PLOTINUS. *Ennead,* ii, 9, 15.

15. Thou wilt become worthy of him. . . . Now a man who was worthy of God would be himself a god.

PORPHYRY. *Letter to Marcella,* xv.

16. O Lord Mazda, grant that through the best righteousness, through the most perfect righteousness, we may catch sight of Thee, may approach Thee, may be united to Thee.

Hush Bam (*Zoroastrian Dawn Hymn*).

17. Being born from out the state of birth-and-death that giveth birth to mortal life, I now, set free, pass to the state transcending birth.

A Mithraic Ritual.

18. I have journeyed from the earth to heaven. The god Shu hath made me to stand up, the god of Light

hath made me to be vigorous by the two sides of the Ladder.

The Egyptian Book of the Dead, xcviii, 4.

19. The man who attains to that place without wrongdoing has an existence there like that of God, going about unhampered like the Everlasting Lords.

The Teaching of King Khati, xiii.

20. The possessor of Tao shall have enduring Life and infinite vision.

LAO TSE.   *Tao Teh King,* lix.

21. The perfect man attains to be without form, and beyond the capability of being transformed.

Kwang Tse, xix, 2.

22. The perfect men of old . . . rambled in the vacancy of Untroubled Ease, found their food in the Fields of Indifference, and stood in gardens which they had not borrowed. The ancients called this the Enjoyment that Collects the True.

Kwang Tse, xiv, 5.

23. Free from impurities, I did attain unto the utter peace of Nirvana. . . . Sure is my release. This is my last birth. There is no more birth for me.

THE BUDDHA.   *Majjhima-Nikaya,* i, 160.

24. We have drunk the Soma, we have become immortal, we have entered into light, we have known the gods.

Rig Veda, viii, 48, 3.

25. When are liberated all the desires that lodge in one's heart, then a mortal becomes immortal. Therein he reaches Brahma.

Katha Upanishad, vi, 14.

26. As the flowing rivers into the ocean disappear, quitting name and form, so the knower, being liberated from name and form, goes into the Heavenly Being, higher than the high.

Mundaka Upanishad, iii, 2, 8.

27. Those, who are free from passion and delusion, who part the bonds constraining them to flesh, ever dwelling in spirit, from whom desire has departed, liberated from the pairs of opposites called pleasure and pain, undeluded pass to the eternal goal.

KRISHNA. *Bhagavad-Gita*, xv, 5.

28. The Dewdrop slips into the shining Sea.

SIR EDWIN ARNOLD. *The Light of Asia*, viii.

29. So shall I fight, so shall I tread,
    In this long war beneath the stars;
So shall a glory wreathe my head,
    So shall I faint and show the scars,
Until this case, this clogging mould,
    Be smithied all to kingly gold.

JOHN MASEFIELD. *A Creed.*

Chronological Table

The beginning of Egypt (from the figures of
    Manetho, Herodotus, etc.) . . . . *Before* 18,000 B.C.
The coming of the Atlanteans against the
    Athenians (according to Plato) . . . . . *c.* 9,400 B.C.
Menes, first historical dynasty of Egypt
    (according to Diodorus) . . . . *c.* 4,700 B.C.
The Egyptian Book of the Dead, Heliopolitan
    Recension; Pyramid Texts . . . . . . *c.* 3,500 B.C.
The beginning of the civilization of Ur . . *c.* 3,500 B.C.
Minoan civilization in Crete . . . . 3,300–1,400 B.C.
Quetzalcoatle of America . . . . *c.* 3,000 B.C.
Fu-hsi, first historical Emperor of China
    (according to Chinese records). . . 2,852–2,738 B.C.
The Teaching of Ptah-hotep . . . . *c.* 2,800 B.C.
The First Dynasty of Babylon. . . . . . *c.* 2,000 B.C.
The Philosophy of Antef. . . . . *c.* 1,800 B.C.
The Theban recension of *The Egyptian*
    Book of the Dead . . . . 1,600–1,000 B.C.
Krishna of India . . . . *c.* 1,500 B.C.
The Hindu *Vedas* . . . . 1,500–1,000 B.C.
The Teaching of Amen-em-apt . . . . . . *c.* 1,400 B.C.
Moses. . . . . *c.* 1,300 B.C.
Zarathushtra (Zoroaster) of Persia . . . . *c.* 1,200 B.C.
The Wisdom of Ani . . . . *c.* 1,000 B.C.
The Persian *Avesta* and *Zend* . . . . . *c.* 1,000–400 B.C.
King Solomon. . . . . *c.* 970 B.C.
Homer . . . . *c.* 900 B.C.
The *Brahmanas* . . . . 800–600 B.C.
The *Upanishads* . . . . *c.* 700–500 B.C.

Isaiah	*c.* 700 B.C.
Lao Tse of China	604–515 B.C.
The *Mahabharata*; the *Sutras*	*c.* 600–200 B.C.
Mahavira, founder of Jainism	*Born c.* 600 B.C.
Pythagoras.	*c.* 572–500 B.C.
Gautama, the Buddha	573–483 B.C.
Confucius	551–479 B.C.
Heracleitus, Greek philosopher	*c.* 500 B.C.
Mo-Tse of China.	*c.* 470–390 B.C.
Socrates	*c.* 470–399 B.C.
Hippocrates, the "Father of Medicine".	*Born c.* 460 B.C.
The *Tipitaka*, the Buddhist canon. . .	*c.* 450–250 B.C.
—Committed to writing	. *c.* 80 B.C.
Plato	429–348 B.C.
Mencius of China	*c.* 370–290 B.C.
Kwang Tse of China	369–286 B.C.
Cleanthes, the Stoic.	331–232 B.C.
The *Septuagint*, Old Testament	280 B.C.
Huai Nan Tse	*Died* 122 B.C.
Virgil, Roman poet	70–19 B.C.
Philo of Alexandria	*c.* 25 B.C.–45 A.D.
Jesus	5 B.C.–30 A.D.
Paul	3–66 A.D.
Apollonius of Tyana	*Died* 97 A.D.
Josephus, Jewish historian	37–98 A.D.
Epictetus, Stoic philosopher	*c.* 50–125 A.D.
Basilides, Greek Gnostic	*c.* 125 A.D.
Marcus Aurelius Antoninus, Roman Emperor.	121–180 A.D.
Valentinus, supposed compiler of *Pistis Sophia*	*c.* 100–170 A.D.
Clement of Alexandria	*c.* 150–216 A.D.

Origen . . . . 185–254 A.D.
Plotinus, Neoplatonic philosopher . . . 204–270 A.D.
Porphyry, Neoplatonic philosopher . . . 233–305 A.D.
Iamblichus . . . . 4th cent. A.D.
The *Codex Sinaiticus*, earliest extant copy
   of the Bible in Greek . . . . *c.* 350 A.D.
The *Vulgate*. . . . . *c.* 400 A.D.
   (The MS. in the British Museum is *c.* 850 A.D.)
The *Codex Alexandrinus* . . . . *c.* 450 A.D.
The Council of Constantinople at which
   belief in reincarnation was first declared
   to be a heresy . . . . 553 A.D.
Mahomet . . . . 570–632 A.D.
The Welsh Triads, first committed to
   writing . . . . *c.* 600 A.D.
Sufism . . . . *From* 8th cent. A.D.
Massoretic Text, the oldest MS. used in
   the translation of the Old Testament . . . 916 A.D.
Kan Ying Phien, the Chinese Tractate of
   Rewards and Punishments . . . . . 11th cent. A.D.
The Albigenses . . . . . 12th and 13th cent. A.D.
Jalalu'd-din Rumi, Persian Sufi Poet . 1207–1273 A.D.
Dante . . . . 1265–1321 A.D.
Christian Rosencreutz (alleged dates) . 1374–1484 A.D.
Baba Nanak, Sikh . . . . 1469–1538 A.D.
Sir Thomas More . . . . 1478–1535 A.D.
Paracelsus, Swiss alchemist . . . . . 1493–1541 A.D.
Coverdale's translation of the Bible . . . . . 1535 A.D.
Shakespeare . . . . 1564–1616 A.D.
Komensky (Comenius), Bohemian . . 1592–1670 A.D.
The Authorized Version of the Bible . . . . 1611 A.D.
Rosicrucian documents, published . . 1615–1616 A.D.
John Bunyan . . . . 1628–1688 A.D.

Karl von Eckartshausen . . . . . .   1752–1813 A.D.
Baha-u-llah (Bahaism). . . . . . .   1817–1892 A.D.
The Revised Version of the Bible   . .   1881–1884 A.D.

Note.—Many of these dates are, of course, not accurately known; they have, nevertheless, been included in the above table in order to show the general sequence.

Bibliography

The Bible and The Apocrypha: Authorized and Revised Versions.

ARNOLD, SIR EDWIN.

The Song Celestial, or Bhagavad-Gita (Kegan Paul, Trench, Trubner & Co., Ltd.).

The Light of Asia (Ditto).

BESTERMAN, T.

In the Way of Heaven (Methuen & Co.).

BUDGE, E. A. WALLIS.

The Book of the Dead (Kegan Paul, Trench, Trubner & Co., Ltd.).

The Teaching of Amen-em-apt (Martin Hopkinson & Co., Ltd.).

BUHLER, G.

The Laws of Manu. Sacred Books of the East series, XXV (The Clarendon Press, Oxford).

BUNYAN, JOHN.

The Pilgrim's Progress (J. M. Dent & Sons, Ltd.).

Grace Abounding (Ditto).

The Holy War (The Society for Promoting Christian Knowledge).

CAMPAGNAC, E. T.

The Way of Light, by John Amos Comenius (Liverpool University Press).

CARY, HENRY.

Dialogues of Plato (Geo. Routledge & Sons, Ltd.).

CASAUBON, M.

The Meditations of Marcus Aurelius (J. M. Dent & Sons, Ltd.).

CHAMPION, S. G.
The Eleven Religions (Geo. Routledge & Sons, Ltd.).

CH'U TA-KAO.
Tao Te Ching (The Buddhist Lodge).

COPE, E. M.
Plato's Gorgias (Geo. Bell & Sons).

CROMBIE, F.
The Writings of Origen (T. & T. Clark).

DANIEL, SIR JOHN.
The Philosophy of Ancient Britain (Williams & Norgate, Ltd.).

DAVIS, H.
Plato's Works (Geo. Bell & Sons).

DODDS, E. R.
Select Passages illustrating Neoplatonism (S.P.C.K.).

ECCLESTON, J., AND R. MONGAN.
The Apology of Socrates, the Crito and the Phaedo (J. Cornish & Sons).

ECKARTSHAUSEN, COUNT KARL VON.
The Cloud upon the Sanctuary (Anonymous translator. Privately printed).

ERMAN, ADOLF (A. M. BLACKMAN, translator).
The Literature of the Ancient Egyptians (Methuen & Co., Ltd.).

FARADAY, WINIFRED.
The Wisdom of the Cymry (The Golden Cockerel Press).

FAUSBÖLL, V.
The Sutta Nipata. Sacred Books of the East series, X (2) (Oxford University Press).

GILES, LIONEL.
The Book of Mencius.
The Sayings of Lao Tzu.
Taoist Teachings (John Murray).

GLANVILLE, S. K. K.

The Legacy of Egypt (The Clarendon Press, Oxford).

HAMMON, E.

The Splendour of God. The Sacred Writings of the Bahais (John Murray).

HARTMANN, F.

The Life of Paracelsus (Kegan Paul, Trench, Trubner & Co., Ltd.).

HAUG, M.

Essays on the Religion of the Parsis (Kegan Paul, Trench, Trubner & Co., Ltd.).

HAYES, WILL.

The Man of Tao (The Order of the Great Companions).

HORNER, GEORGE.

The Pistis Sophia (S.P.C.K.).

HUGHES, E. R.

Chinese Philosophy in Classical Times.

The Great Learning and The Mean in Action (J. M. Dent & Sons, Ltd.).

HUME, R. E.

The Thirteen Principal Upanishads (Oxford University Press).

JAMES, M. R.

The Apocryphal New Testament (The Clarendon Press, Oxford).

JAYASUNDERE, A. D.

The Numerical Sayings (Anguttara-Nikaya) (The Vesanta Press, Madras).

JOWETT, B.

The Dialogues of Plato (The Clarendon Press, Oxford).

KINGSLAND, W.

An Anthology of Mysticism (Methuen & Co., Ltd.).

KIPLING, RUDYARD.

Songs from Books.

The Naulahka.
Puck of Pook's Hill (Macmillan & Co. Ltd., and with permission of Mrs. George Bambridge).

LEGGE, J.
Texts of Taoism. Sacred Books of the East series, XXXIX and XL (Oxford University Press).

LINDSAY, A. D.
Plato's Republic (J. M. Dent & Sons, Ltd.).

LONGFELLOW, H. W.
The Song of Hiawatha (Blackie & Son, Ltd.).

LUTZOW, COUNT.
The Labyrinth of the World, by J. A. Komensky (J. M. Dent & Sons, Ltd.).

LYALL, L. A.
Mencius (Longmans Green & Co., Ltd.).

MACNICOL, N.
Hindu Scriptures (J. M. Dent & Sons, Ltd.).

MALPAS, P. A.
The Popol Vuh (*The Theosophical Path*, March 1930, ff.).

MARTIN, EVA.
The Ring of Return (Philip Allan & Co.).

MASEFIELD, J.
Collected Poems (W. Heinemann, by permission of the Society of Authors and Dr. John Masefield, O.M.).

MASINI, R. P.
The Religion of the Good Life (Geo. Allen & Unwin, Ltd.).

MEAD, G. R. S.
Fragments of a Faith Forgotten (John M. Watkins).
The Chaldean Oracles.
A Mithraic Ritual.
The Mysteries of Mythra (The Theosophical Publishing Society).

MEARS, ISABELLA.

Tao Teh King, by Lao Tzu (The Theosophical Publishing House).

MORE, SIR THOMAS.

Utopia (Geo. Bell & Sons, Ltd.).

MOULTON, J. H.

The Treasure of the Magi (H. Milford, Oxford University Press).

MÜLLER, MAX.

The Dhammapada. Sacred Books of the East series, X (1) (Oxford University Press).

OLD, W. G.

Lao Tse (Rider & Co.).

PALEY, F. A.

The Philebus of Plato (Geo. Bell & Sons).

POTTER, C.

The Divina Commedia of Dante (Digby, Long & Co.).

ROLLESTON, T. W.

The Teaching of Epictetus (George Routledge & Sons, Ltd.).

RUTTER, OWEN.

The Scales of Karma (Andrew Dakers, Ltd.).

Sacred Books of the East, Described and Examined (The Christian Literature Society for India).

SHRINE OF WISDOM SERIES:

The Simple Way of Lao Tze.
The History of Great Light.
Two Dialogues of Plato.

SPENS, H.

The Republic of Plato (J. M. Dent & Sons, Ltd.).

SWARUPANANDA, SWAMI.

Simad Bhagavad-Gita (Swami Pavitrananda Advaita Ashrama).

TAYLOR, TH.
  Select Works of Plotinus (Geo. Bell & Sons, Ltd.).

THOMAS, E. J.
  Early Buddhist Scriptures (Kegan Paul, Trench, Trubner & Co., Ltd.).

TIDDEMAN, M. F.
  A Short Life of Apollonius of Tyana (The Theosophical Publishing House).

(VARIOUS.)
  Plato: Five Dialogues (J. M. Dent & Sons, Ltd.).

WAITE, A. E.
  The Real History of the Rosicrucians (George Redway).

WATERHOUSE, J. W.
  Zoroastrianism (The Epworth Press).

WATSON, SIR WILLIAM.
  The Poems of Sir William Watson, 1878–1935 (George G. Harrap & Co., Ltd.).

WATTERS, H.
  The Pythagorean Way of Life (The Theosophical Publishing House).

WHISTON, W.
  The Works of Flavius Josephus (William Milner).

WISDOM OF THE EAST SERIES:
  Musings of a Chinese Mystic.
  The Persian Mystics.

WOODWARD, F. L.
  Some Sayings of the Buddha (Oxford University Press).

ZIMMERN, ALICE.
  Porphyry (The Priory Press).

Grateful acknowledgment is made for the above books as sources of quotations.

THIS EXCLUSIVE EDITION
*has been typeset for The Reincarnation Library
in Caslon, Bulmer, and Bell, and printed by fine-line
offset lithography on archival quality paper at
Thomson-Shore, Inc.
The text and end-papers are acid-free and
meet or surpass all guidelines established
by the Council of Library Resources
and the American National
Standards Institute™.*

―――――――

Book design by Jerry Kelly.

WISDOM IS ONE
By B. W. Huntsman

Here is a fascinating compilation of quotations from some of history's most renowned philosophers, thinkers and teachers, covering Reincarnation, as well as many other subjects which relate to certain fundamental questions of life.

Painstakingly gathered and assembled in this unique collection, the quotations are organized under various subject headings, such as The Law of Reincarnation, The Law of Karma, Knowledge and Truth, Evolution and Attainment, etc. Hundreds of quotations from sources as far apart as *The Egyptian Book of The Dead* to Rudyard Kipling, reveal the abundance of thought on these age-old ideas. Free of any commentary, the quotations themselves demonstrate a striking similarity of thought by a widely diverse group of individuals.

Whether you keep this book handy to pick out favorite quotations, or read it from cover to cover, you'll find it to be thought provoking, practical and enlightening.